"Dennis Edwards eloquently wri[...] humility 'brings truth's light by throwing back the shutters of arrogance and opening the window of curiosity.' Similarly, this wonderful book—by someone who embodies its subject—offers a window into the multifaceted Christian identity marker of humility before God and others, throwing back the shutters of distortion and misunderstanding. Well-researched, wise, and highly readable, this is a timely book for all Christians in an age of competition, self-promotion, and division."

Michael J. Gorman, Raymond E. Brown Professor of Biblical Studies and Theology at St. Mary's Seminary & University in Baltimore, Maryland

"In *Humility Illuminated*, Dennis R. Edwards elevates the practice and power of humility as a central indicator of a sincere Christ-follower. In providing a careful exploration of the complexities of humility, Edwards gives his readers a grounded trajectory to follow that is both fresh and robust, leading to faithful practice. Infused with astute biblical analysis and proficient pastoral experience, Edwards is a practitioner of humility who the church ought to follow."

Rose Lee-Norman, executive pastor at Sanctuary Covenant Church in Minneapolis, Minnesota, and adjunct professor of reconciliation studies at Bethel University

"In *Humility Illuminated*, Dennis R. Edwards challenges us to move beyond the trappings of church and live into the example of Jesus. This book serves as an invitation to let American competitiveness fall by the wayside as we embrace the humble posture of the marginalized among us. Sitting with these words reminds us that if Jesus is the way, the truth, and the life, humility is the safest path to godly community."

R. G. A. "Trey" Ferguson, cohost of *Three Black Men* podcast and author of *Theologizin' Bigger*

"Edwards points out that Christian humility is not episodic but a whole way of life, a vital necessity for the life of discipleship. Humility is much misunderstood and misapplied as self-hatred, as 'humble bragging,' as passivity. Edwards strikingly paints a picture of Jesus-centered humility as singular devotion to God, a posture of peacemaking with others, and the quiet power to seek justice for everyone made in God's image. By the end of the book, it dawned on me, humility is maturity."

Nijay K. Gupta, professor of New Testament at Northern Seminary

"Our ultracompetitive culture encourages us to outstrip others in quests for social status and prestige, and these temptations affect individual Christians and the ethos of church communities. In *Humility Illuminated*, Dennis Edwards provides a rich treatment of how Scripture prizes humility as both internal disposition and social practice. He draws on his many years of pastoral experience to wisely counsel readers on how to follow Jesus in the way of humility, which enriches our common humanity, connects us intimately to others, and generates hope."

Timothy Gombis, author of *Power in Weakness: Paul's Transformed Vision for Ministry*

Dennis R. Edwards

humility illuminated

the biblical path back to christian character

Foreword by Marlena Graves

IVP Academic
An imprint of InterVarsity Press
Downers Grove, Illinois

InterVarsity Press
P.O. Box 1400 | Downers Grove, IL 60515-1426
ivpress.com | email@ivpress.com

InterVarsity Press® is the publishing division of InterVarsity Christian Fellowship/USA®. For more information, visit intervarsity.org.

Cover design: David Fassett
Interior design: Daniel van Loon
Images: Getty 157523656 Cover Image Abstract Painting: © philsajonesen / Getty Images

ISBN 978-1-5140-0044-1 (print) | ISBN 978-1-5140-0045-8 (digital)

Printed in the United States of America ♾

Library of Congress Cataloging-in-Publication Data
A catalog record for this book is available from the Library of Congress.

30 29 28 27 26 25 24 23 | 13 12 11 10 9 8 7 6 5 4 3 2 1

For my wife, Susan Steele Edwards, and our children,

Jonathan, Jason, Joanna, and Jessica.

You've witnessed my journey and still love me.

GLORY TO GOD!

And for the many unsung heroes who serve God faithfully

yet don't receive public recognition.

GOD SEES YOU!

Contents

Foreword

Marlena Graves

Humility is the gateway to all the other virtues, the early church fathers and mothers tell us. That being the case, one would assume that *humble* is a word that comes to mind whenever we hear the word *Christian* bandied about. Unfortunately, such is often not the case here in the United States—at least among most of the Christian leaders who have the mic and spotlight. Indeed, it is often those who have charisma, the "it factor," money, good looks, or big churches who appear to rule the day and others. The humble? Overlooked. For the most part, humility is seen as weakness in a dog-eat-dog world and church. The church in the United States often mirrors our culture much more than we would like to admit. And that's where we have it all wrong. That's where we are way off course.

In *Humility Illuminated: The Biblical Path Back to Christian Character*, the Reverend Dr. Dennis R. Edwards seeks to offer us a course correction. Humility, he tells us, directly corresponds to our intimacy with God and our subsequent obedience to God. Moses was the humblest man on the earth because of his intimacy with God (and purification in the wilderness). An intimate relationship with the Lord can't help but lead us to humility. And so, when I look at many of our leaders and those of us in church, I wonder whether we are spending time with God. If humility is indicative of our intimacy with God, then it seems the answer must be that we are not. Edwards calls us back to the way of Jesus, to the way of Philippians 2. Jesus was so intimate with, and reliant on the Father and Holy Spirit that he was the humblest human being ever to exist. He was so humble and so invested in others that he took on the role of a slave serving all, though he should have been, and should be, served by all.

Humility ought to characterize me, our Christian communities, our worship, and our interactions with those who are different from us. Edwards writes, "Being humble is not meant to be episodic but rather an abiding and ever-developing aspect of Christian life." We are to embody humility more and more as we become more intimate with the Lord. Yet Edwards does not merely exhort us to follow Jesus' way of humility; he humbly shows us how to do it in a wise scholar-pastor fashion.

One of the things I most appreciated about this book is that Edwards reminds us that we do not seek humility *to achieve the status* of the greatest in the kingdom of God, but rather that the humblest *are* the greatest people in the kingdom of God. Furthermore, I thought it quite brilliant, wise, and true that humility is what will bring healing to our church and world, as Edwards asserts. I never thought about it that way before, and it is something that I will continue to turn over and over in my mind—and hopefully embody more and more! That humility can't help but flow from our love of God and people.

I am going to be honest with you. It grates me to no end when people who are so obviously not humble wax eloquent on humility or are appointed as Christian leaders. And then we wonder why people have such a bad taste in their mouth when they think of the church in the United States. It's because humility is so rare. Not so with Dennis Edwards. It strikes me as quite ironic that such an extremely accomplished person—a musician, athlete, New

Testament scholar, pastor, preacher with a BS in chemical engineering from Cornell, former high school teacher, and currently dean of North Park Seminary and vice president of church relations who has sat on boards of organizations—is writing about humility. It strikes me as ironic because as an African American man, he and his ancestors know continual humiliation at the hands of those who have wielded, and continue to wield, power in the US. And still, he calls us to be humble. Here he is, and here we are, holding this treasure of a book from a brother who is so accomplished and yet speaking from the margins, not the top of the hierarchy.

The way of Jesus is most often embodied and communicated by those on the margins, from those who depend on God alone for who they are. This is why I can trust the content of this book. Edwards embodies humility. He is a true leader and surely among the greatest in the kingdom of God. Not because he is so accomplished in the world's eyes, but because he is so humble, which is indicative of his intimacy with God. His humility and our humility garner God's favor. For God resists the proud but gives grace to the humble (Jas 4:4-7). So as we collectively take heed of Edwards's words, we will begin to look more and more like Jesus to both those inside and those outside the church.

Dennis is an expert and reliable guide. I am honored to sit at his feet and learn. May we be countercultural even in the church as we grow in humility. Thank you, Reverend Dr. Edwards, for showing us the way!

Acknowledgments

Shortly after moving to Illinois, I had the privilege of connecting with Jeff Crosby (former IVP publisher), whom I had met previously at a conference, and with former IVP Academic editor Anna Moseley Gissing. Jeff and Anna each affirmed how my writing reflects both my academic and pastoral experiences. I'm grateful for associate publisher and academic editorial director Jon Boyd, who helped shepherd this book to publication.

I earned my PhD in biblical studies at a time when there were relatively few African American biblical scholars in the country, but I did not move right away into a full-time academic position. I opted instead to teach as an adjunct instructor while remaining a pastor in Washington, DC. Washington became home for nearly eighteen years after moving from Brooklyn, New York, where I started New Community Church in our family's apartment. After serving several years at Washington Community Fellowship Church on Capitol Hill, I planted Peace Fellowship Church in a neighborhood east of the Anacostia River. I concluded my years of pastoral ministry after serving six years as senior pastor of the Sanctuary Covenant Church in Minneapolis, Minnesota. I mention these churches because they taught me about God and about myself and helped me to mature as a servant of God.

Two men I met in Washington have been especially helpful, not only with regard to this book, but with much of my life. I love

Rev. Randy Heacock and Ben Byerly. These brothers in the faith embody the humility I attempt to describe throughout this book. Their love and support continue to provoke me in my efforts to demonstrate love and do good deeds, as the writer of Hebrews admonishes (Heb 10:24).

I acknowledge the North Park Theological Seminary community. My faculty and staff colleagues, along with the students, continually enrich my life through their faith, service, and love for God's people. Special acknowledgment goes to my predecessor, David Kersten, to the current dean of faculty, Hauna Ondrey, and to New Testament professor Max Lee for their continual affirmation and encouragement. Also among the seminary community is my research assistant, Lynnea Miller, whom I acknowledge for joyfully and skillfully helping with my various writing projects.

Finally, I acknowledge my wife, Susan Steele Edwards, who consistently cheers me on and—for some reason—enjoys proofreading my work! However, I am solely responsible for any inaccuracies or errors in this book.

Introduction

Rediscovering Humility for Our Times

Toward the scorners he is scornful,
but to the humble he shows favor.

PROVERBS 3:34

THE CHURCH IN THE UNITED STATES—AND perhaps in other places throughout the world—needs to recover, respect, and reenact biblical humility. We Christians are fractured, but humility will help us to heal. Our world has always been fragmented, and Christians are not immune to the forces that drive wedges between people. But we seem to be at a critical juncture that requires fresh solutions to age-old problems. Churches are increasingly polarized because of politics, and many pastors are at their wits' end trying to discern how to love people well while denouncing misinformation, sexism, racism, and other forms of injustice. The rhetoric from many professing Christians demeans weak, marginalized, humiliated people—the very ones God calls us to honor and serve. Influenced by the surrounding culture,

Christians' words and actions are often prouder and more scornful than humble, gentle, and teachable.

The Black Lives Matter movement, for example, continues to draw attention to racial injustice, while some—even Christians—try to discredit or ignore the movement rather than honestly explore the reasons for racial injustice and the need for Black Lives Matter's existence. The MeToo movement put a spotlight on the sexual violence and harassment embedded within societal structures, which threatens the safety and well-being of our mothers, sisters, daughters, colleagues, and friends. Such movements expose how society's institutions and systems have been built on a foundation of racism, classism, sexism, and nationalism. But it has become nearly impossible to have meaningful conversations about these realities.

As a prime example, some leaders and institutions have turned critical race theory into a bogeyman designed to frighten their constituents into banning the academic field of study instead of engaging with it. Through inaccurate descriptions and sensational accusations, critical race theory is presented as a menacing specter hovering over vulnerable children. Actually, truth about the theory is often shrouded in the darkness of ignorance, and many—mostly White—Christians are agitated because anxiety is confusion's companion.

Humility brings truth's light by throwing back the shutters of arrogance and opening the window of curiosity. With these hot-button issues and others, curious people ask questions. And with more answers—or at least investigation—we move toward understanding. The journey toward understanding can reduce fears, fortify faith, and allow love to flourish. Humility makes us curious, guiding us onward to love, and with love we can heal.

The church's growing irrelevance in parts of the United States as well as some other places in the world is not because Christianity has lost its brain but because it seems to have lost its heart.

Increasing numbers of PhD graduates in Bible, theology, and related fields testify to Christianity's brainpower, but the inability of many of these graduates to secure employment in their discipline points to a different problem. We have fewer people attending churches, and church people are a major funding source for Christian institutions. Consequently, divinity schools and theological seminaries are struggling—unless they are well-endowed, historic institutions attached to large universities.

Increasing numbers of people reject Christianity despite the energy expended to evangelize, to explain the Bible, and to offer answers to people's pressing questions about life. One piece of evidence of the church's heart loss is the way many Christians make it hard for unbelievers to recognize Jesus. Ironically, arrogance rather than humility often accompanies erudition—the more information we amass, the less we seem to be able to empathize with others. Academics and other church leaders focused for centuries on what we might call *theological* or *doctrinal* matters, putting ink to paper or voice to soapbox in attempts to clarify biblical truths for each other. Meanwhile, onlookers scratched their heads, averted their gaze, and bolted in a different direction.

Doctrinal clarity surely has a place, but as the adage says, "People won't care how much you know till they know how much you care." A clear way to show how much we care is to be open, honest, vulnerable, approachable, and generally unafraid of listening rather than talking. Humility allows us to have a posture that invites rather than repels.

Humility Is a Christian Identity Marker

What is humility, and why is it essential for Christians? These are questions we will explore throughout this book. Humility is a way of life rooted in submission to God and is demonstrated in actions that foster mutuality rather than competition. Humility is a biblical virtue, though it has often been misunderstood both inside and outside the church.

Eve-Marie Becker contends that "in early Christianity humility was regarded as a virtue that was unknown in the pagan world" and "thus as a Christian identity marker."[1] She references Augustine, who frequently mentions humility, and also a homily of fourth-century Pseudo-Macarius, who takes humility as "a sign of what is Christian."[2] In the first few centuries after the resurrection of Jesus Christ, his followers could be identified by their humility.

This might prompt us to wonder what identifies Christians in our time. To some onlookers, bigotry, stinginess, racism, patriarchy, homophobia, nationalism, and hypocrisy are among the signifiers of Christians in the United States. But even if we aren't that cynical, we might confess that there is only an ambiguous witness to those observing Christian faith when it comes to humility. As much as we might nod in agreement that humility is important and necessary, we struggle to practice it.

My dearest friend, a fellow pastor, has wondered aloud with me whether the Christian struggle to practice humility is because we generally abhor vulnerability. The church is often the last place where we can confess our sins to one another and pray for each other so that we can all be healed (see Jas 5:16). There are always exceptions to what my friend and I have observed in our combined sixty-five or so years of Christian ministry, but we are not far from the mark. Many of us might struggle to practice humility because we misunderstand it as a sign of weakness, even though we give lip service to the contrary.

[1]Eve-Marie Becker, *Paul on Humility*, trans. Wayne Coppins, Baylor–Mohr Siebeck Studies in Early Christianity (Waco, TX: Baylor University Press, 2020), 28.

[2]Becker, *Paul on Humility*, 28-29. Augustine writes of how Jesus hides wisdom from people the world considers clever so they would turn to the Lord "since he is gentle and humble of heart; and with his judgments of what's right he will guide those who are gentle, and he teaches the meek to walk in his ways." *Confessions*, trans. Sarah Ruden (New York: Modern Library, 2018), 7.14. Becker quotes from Pseudo-Marcarius, *Homily* 15.27.

Jane Foulcher states, "While humility had a central place in early Christian theology and practice, it has generally been marginalized by the modern Western world and in contemporary Christian life."[3] Foulcher is one of several authors who note that Scottish philosopher David Hume dismissed humility as a "monkish virtue," and German philosopher Friedrich Nietzsche referred to humility as Christian "slave morality" that demonized the pursuit of power and self-fulfillment.[4] There is also a stream within Christianity that distorts humility by equating it with humiliation and smallness.

For example, in his book *Humility* the mystic Andrew Murray consistently presses readers to view themselves as insignificant, going so far as to say, "Accept every humiliation, look upon every fellow-man who tries or vexes you, as a means of grace to humble you."[5] In light of Murray's context, however, this advice is problematic. Murray appears to have been instrumental in setting the stage for apartheid in South Africa by introducing a resolution in the Dutch Reformed Church for racially separate congregations.[6] Given Murray's perspective on segregation, he seemed to be chiefly concerned about the vexation that White people received. The oppressed Blacks of South Africa surely did not need to be told that what Whites were doing to them was God's way of humbling them. Murray's perspective on humility does not address the power differentials in society—some of which Christians either created or supported. Yet true humility means movement toward justice rather than away from it.

Humility's bad reputation has made many of us wary of becoming doormats. Consequently, most speakers and writers are

---

[3]Jane Foulcher, *Reclaiming Humility: Four Studies in the Monastic Tradition*, Cistercian Studies 255 (Collegeville, MN: Cistercian Publications, 2015), xx.

[4]Foulcher, *Reclaiming Humility*, xx. Also, Lanier Burns, *Pride and Humility at War: A Biblical Perspective* (Phillipsburg, NJ: P&R, 2018), 10; Reinhard Feldmeier, *Power, Service, Humility: A New Testament Ethic* (Waco, TX: Baylor University Press, 2014), 64; Becker, *Paul on Humility*, 14.

[5]Andrew Murray, *Humility* (Springdale, PA: Whitaker House, 1982), 45.

[6]See John Scheepers, "How Did Our 'Good Evangelical Theology' Allow Apartheid?," Isiphambano Centre for Biblical Justice, October 22, 2018, www.isiphambano.com/blog/how-did-our-good-evangelical-theology-allow-apartheid.

quick to distinguish humility from self-deprecation.[7] Yet this can lead to other kinds of distortion. John Dickson is about as far from Andrew Murray as one can get, selling humility as beneficial for success in our society: "My thesis is simple: *The most influential and inspiring people are often marked by humility*."[8] Dickson goes on to present humility as a quintessential American value, offering exemplars from the worlds of business, sports, and the military—the usual trinity invoked as inspiration for church leaders in our nation.

Perspectives like that of Andrew Murray present humility as self-loathing, while views like that of Dickson present humility as a stepping stone for upward mobility in our competitive society. Since both of those views appear to me as distortions, I find Reinhard Feldmeier's viewpoint helpful: "When we speak of humility, we must always bear in mind these possibilities that the idea of humility may be distorted and abused; these possibilities are probably as old as the concept itself."[9] Perhaps our eagerness and care to present humility in a positive light comes out of our fear of being devalued more than our fear of devaluing others. Popular presentations of humility encourage us to avoid some of the pitfalls of personal pride, but they come off like self-help books for us to live our best lives in a comfortable middle- to upper-class American neighborhood. These presentations might exhort us to go low—just not *too* low. We fear that humility will weaken us rather than empower us, so we give greater energy to self-preservation than to collaboration. Even Christians adopt slogans

---

[7]Christopher Hutchinson, *Rediscovering Humility: Why the Way Up Is Down* (Greensboro, NC: New Growth Press, 2018), 16-18, is one of many who decry self-deprecation early in their work. Dan Kent, *Confident Humility: Becoming Your Full Self Without Becoming Full of Yourself* (Minneapolis, MN: Fortress, 2018) does well to explain the need to avoid "the Ditch of Smallness" or self-loathing despite its "seductive charms" (esp. 8-13).

[8]John P. Dickson, *Humilitas: A Lost Key to Life, Love, and Leadership* (Grand Rapids, MI: Zondervan, 2011), 19 (emphasis original).

[9]Feldmeier, *Power, Service, Humility*, 64-65.

like "Look out for number one," or "America first," and we can find Bible verses to protect our self-interests.

Feldmeier offers more wisdom here: "The controversial character of humility is not only due to the history of its abuse. Another factor is that, like service, humility too demands of the human being something that accords only to a very limited degree with his nature, which is programmed to promote self-assertion."[10] Human nature focuses on personal advancement, and even the words of Jesus in Luke 18:14 ("for all who exalt themselves will be humbled, but all who humble themselves will be exalted") can paradoxically be construed as a strategy for worldly success.[11] Humility is not about personal fulfilment, however, but about fulfilling God's desires through the formation of communal bonds with God and others.

Without humility there is no justice. A lack of humility means that the vulnerable in society will continue to suffer. Rather than fear becoming doormats, we should instead become agitated that too many people already are. Humility opens our eyes to the needs of others and is more than a step on our journey of self-actualization.

All Christian teachings get twisted, but we must not let our understanding of humility (or any other biblical topic) be a mere reaction against ignorance or exegetical malpractice. Instead, we need to continually let our thinking be shaped by Scripture, the best of Christian tradition, and the transforming work of the Holy Spirit. There is sort of a cottage industry—or at least it appears so on social media—of knocking other people's ideas. Healthy disagreement is necessary, but demonizing those with whom we

---

[10] Feldmeier, *Power, Service, Humility*, 65.

[11] Foulcher, *Reclaiming Humility*, 129, observes how in the writings of Saint Benedict, "*humilitatis* began to look like a commodity." She goes on to say, "For a contemporary, achievement-focused culture, there is a danger that the ladder of humility might be read as a step-machine, where one sweats out a prescribed program to achieve spiritual fitness—or, worse, an escalator bringing one speedily and effortlessly to the top floor, so that there is a sort of inevitability regarding the outcome."

disagree can hardly be the Lord's strategy for the unity of Christ followers. I hope that we can shift energy away from denouncing others and channel it into inquiry, dialogue, and shared action—reclaiming biblical humility as a Christian way of being.

Humility Is a Way of Life

People are competitive, constantly scrutinizing each other to discover others' weaknesses. For good reason, such as the experience of having been exploited on occasion, many of us resist appearing vulnerable. We avoid sharing personal details and are careful not to display any shortcomings. Therefore, to protect our psyches as well as our bodies, we develop a version of humility in which we do not yield much ground to others but simultaneously avoid accusations of arrogance. Yet, rather than trying to either absolve ourselves of pride or present a glittering image of success to the world, we would do better to resist society's hierarchical, competitive culture and humbly examine why we feel the need for self-promotion. Embracing humility does not begin with worries about how others might perceive me. I do not need to measure or calculate my humility as if I am being graded on some sort of scale. We don't need to prove how humble we are—it isn't a contest. Humility grows from my relationship with God and governs how I interact with other people. Cultivating humility means pursuing intimacy with God and compassionately serving others without worrying about my brand or stressing over my popularity. The resounding refrain throughout Scripture and Christian noncanonical writings is that God opposes the arrogant while being gracious to the humble (see Prov 3:34). Humility exhorts me to trust God's grace rather than be anxious about my worldly status.

I was anxious about my status in the world after it became evident that the church I had started in our tiny Brooklyn apartment was not going to survive. Along with innumerable pragmatic concerns about how I'd make a living as a husband with four children, I was also plagued with feelings of inadequacy, figuring I had failed as a church planter and pastor. I had much more to learn about humility. Eventually I found myself at a church in Washington, DC, interviewing for an associate pastor position. During one of the interview sessions, a church leader queried, "What attribute of Jesus stands out to you the most?" Initially, I did not appreciate being asked to rank aspects of the Lord's character, and I am still not comfortable with the question. But I responded with the first word that came to mind: "humility." I continued my answer by reflecting on how Philippians 2:5-11 presents a humble Jesus and informs the way I try to embody my Christian faith.

Nearly twenty-five years after that interview, I was installed as a seminary faculty member alongside another newcomer to the institution. A few days prior to the ceremony, we each had been asked to submit a favorite passage from the Bible, and as the attendees stood for the Scripture readings, everyone learned—including the two of us—that we had each selected the same passage: Philippians 2:5-11. Over the next several months I observed ways that my colleague embodies humility in the spirit of this passage.

Although I have long desired to practice humility as a way of life, I have not always thought deeply about what it is. I relied on assumptions and popular notions without examining the Scriptures. In my thinking, humility has been a mixed bag of behaviors, including self-deprecation, secretive good deeds, deflecting praise, refraining from using or being addressed by earned titles, reluctance to pursue prominent positions, shining the spotlight onto others, submitting to the leadership of unqualified supervisors, not saying anything negative—even if true—about another person, suppressing my desires in hopes of harmony, and being the first in line to do menial tasks. Not everything in that mixed bag is unhealthy or bad, but it's not all good either. While I cannot point to one specific turning point in my understanding, I can see that throughout decades of ministry, I continually reflected on the notion of humility and know that it is not merely *being nice*.

Humility doesn't sanction rudeness, but neither does it require rejecting God-given talents, abilities, gifts, ideas, and perspectives. Humility means being grounded, having an accurate self-perception that is neither too high nor too low, shaped by an intimate relationship with God. *Grounded* is an apt term because it reminds us that *humble*, *humility*, and *humiliation* derive from *humus*, the Latin word for "earth" or "ground." People who are humble are level with the ground, but those who are humiliated get crushed into the ground. But it is the faith and tenacity of the humiliated that teaches us what authentic humility entails. The lowly show us the way of Christ.

Lowly should not be confused with *small* or *insignificant*. Andrew Murray's perspective leads him to exclaim,

> Humility is our being, in God's presence, nothing but a speck dwelling in the sunlight of His love. How great is God! how small am I! Lost, swallowed up in Love's immensity! God only there, not I. May God teach us to believe that to be humble, to be nothing in His presence, is the highest attainment, and the fullest blessing of the Christian life.[12]

We might appreciate Murray's enthusiasm for God's overwhelming, all-consuming presence, and his desire that we submit ourselves entirely to God. However, *speck*, *small*, and *nothing* are contrary to how God wants us to view ourselves. The biblical language of humility includes a variety of words that can refer to societal status, but *speck*, *small*, and *nothing* connote minimal or no inherent worth. We are, on the contrary, as the old children's song

[12]Murray, *Humility*, 95.

celebrates, precious in God's sight, being "fearfully and wonderfully made" (Ps 139:14), shaped in God's image, and so divinely loved that Jesus, the unique Son of God, died for us (Jn 3:16). We never need to devalue ourselves or others, even when assuming a low position.

The Trajectory of Biblical Humility

Humility is not meant to be episodic, where distinct actions are assigned the label *humble*. Humility is instead a way of life, and the Bible explicates humility by portraying its operation. Biblical humility has a trajectory like a projectile, which I attempt to trace throughout this book.[13] Humility's trajectory begins with submission to God and moves to embodiment in all areas of life, including the creation and strengthening of Christian community. We gain an expanding vision of this movement as we study humility across the Old Testament, the life of Jesus, and the early church.

In chapter one I focus on the Old Testament, exploring words and images related to humility and its companion, meekness, starting with the example of Moses. Humility begins as yielding to God. As we submit to God, we demonstrate ways that humility defines our character. In the popular understanding, humility is not restricted to Christian or other religious faith and practice, but the Bible treats our relationship with God as the basis of humility.

The Lord Jesus Christ is the ultimate example of humility, and in chapter two I examine the life and teachings of the Lord as presented in the Gospels and Philippians 2, demonstrating how humility must be embodied as a way of life. While all the Gospels provide helpful pictures of Jesus' humility, for the sake of focus I rely chiefly on Matthew's Gospel to examine humility in the Lord's

---

[13]Dickson, *Humilitas*, 100-101, describes our "journey" to understand humility from the Old Testament, to Sirach, and then to New Testament portraits of Jesus. That journey is not linear, but more like parabolic upward movement—the arc of a projectile.

words and actions. Paul's writings are the earliest New Testament documents, and the way he employs the language of humility differs from how other Greco-Roman writers use the same words. Paul helps us to see what makes humility godly.

In chapter three I show how indispensable humility is for establishing and maintaining Christian community. Communities built on love are the ultimate apologetic for the Christian faith, and humility is how that love blossoms. Communing is critical, but without humility we delude ourselves into thinking that bonds between Christian siblings are stronger than they really are.

Of course, conflict arises even within tight-knit groups. Disagreements and disputes are an inevitable part of all communities, and they have also been the source of explosive divisions. In chapter four, humility is foregrounded as a key ingredient for negotiating conflict. Humility ought to characterize not only those engaged in conflict but also those who attempt to help feuding factions find harmony.

In chapter five I put leaders in the spotlight because they often set the tone for their communities. Consequently, *humble leaders* cannot be an oxymoron despite the awards our world gives to those who exploit competition, or the pressure society places on leaders to be dictatorial.

My three decades of pastoral experience prompted me to also highlight the role of humility in arenas that are often taken for granted or treated at surface level. Suffering (the focus of chapter six), like conflict, is inevitable. The so-called prosperity gospel has served to minimize or even negate the reality of suffering. Yet the prosperity preachers aren't the only ones who miss suffering's potentially redemptive role. Many of us rely on platitudes—such as "everything happens for a reason" or "God is allowing you to suffer because your faith is so great"—when we are suffering, or we offer them to sisters and brothers who are struggling. These are not helpful. People who suffer, as well as those who witness suffering, can find that humility does not offer easy answers, but offers supernatural insight into what a relationship with God truly means. Humility helps us look upward in the midst of suffering, finding strength to endure or perhaps even to escape our predicament.

We take for granted that Christians are to worship, but we usually refer primarily to singing together. Singing, along with some other aspects of a church's celebratory worship service, are the source of continual debates, divisions, and distortions in Christian community life. In chapter seven I emphasize humility's influence in governing our definitions and depictions of Christian worship.

Another aspect of Christian experience that tends to be taken for granted is making financial contributions. In some circles, the argument surrounds how much should be given (e.g., a literal *tithe* of 10 percent and whether that should be calculated according to gross or net pay). The New Testament places much more emphasis on the *how* and *why* of financial giving than on *how much*. But making financial contributions is not all that stewardship entails. Chapter eight reveals how humility must characterize our stewardship in every area of life.

If humility entails some degree of giving up or giving away our personal power or agency, then it would appear to weaken rather than strengthen us. If humility means weakening, then we do well to wonder why any clear-thinking person should pursue it. In chapter nine, I discuss how humility empowers Jesus followers, even those whom society marginalizes or alienates.

Throughout this book, I combine evidence from the biblical texts with insights from my own experience as a pastor, professor, and church member. Furthermore, as a member of a minoritized group in the United States, I bring a vantage point to humility that those with a more privileged perspective might miss. For example, privileged members of our society might understand humility to include performing occasional charitable acts while I view humility as upsetting the status quo so as to create equitable systems. In my way of thinking, humility is not a formula to achieve the so-called American dream, but is a Jesus-shaped pathway that reflects God's grace.

Marlena Graves, in *The Way Up Is Down: Becoming Yourself by Forgetting Yourself*, puts a spotlight on the humility of Jesus and what it means for us:

> In the midst of his volitional poverty during his life and death on earth, we see he learned humility—to completely depend on God and also on others. He had to. After all he suffered because of what he gave up to become fully human (while being fully God), he continues to wash the feet of his friends and enemies alike. Jesus, the God of the universe, rich as he is in every conceivable and inconceivable manner, washes my feet. And your feet. Even now, no place is too low for Jesus to stoop in order to serve others. Behold the humility of God.[14]

Humility offers us an opportunity for fresh experiences of God's presence and power. Humility opens us anew to the Holy Spirit's movement within us and through us. Rather than Christians trying to find ways to accommodate society's anti-humility, arrogant, selfish, and vainglorious tendencies, we must adopt a different perspective. We must follow a different pathway. We need to traverse humility's trajectory.

[14]Marlena Graves, *The Way Up Is Down: Becoming Yourself by Forgetting Yourself* (Downers Grove, IL: InterVarsity Press, 2020), 19.

Chapter One

Yielding

Where Humility Starts

And God brings the proud to nought,
and exalts the meek and humble.

LETTER OF ARISTEAS 236

THE UNITED STATES IS A COMPETITIVE SOCIETY. We hold contests for almost everything, ranging from identifying the most conventionally beautiful people, to discovering chefs who can whip up delicacies from unknown ingredients in a limited amount of time, to rewarding racers who are the fastest at driving cars in circles. More significantly, we see that wealth, physical strength, and political and social connections grant access to the rarefied air of the upper strata of our nation's hierarchy. But unless a scandal makes it newsworthy, we rarely know the full story of how the elites gained their wealth, power, and influence. We know athletes have used performance-enhancing substances only because of some heroes who were knocked off their pedestals. In some cases, families exploited people and policies for generations. The socially well-connected often benefit from the marginalization of others.

The United States' competitiveness, especially as it relates to social status, is reminiscent of the honor-shame contrasts of the ancient world. In ancient times as well as in the contemporary United States, people of lower status exist to serve the needs of those of higher status.[1] Members within competitive societies do not take their social cues, by and large, or learn their valuable life lessons from those in relatively lower positions. "In the competitive society of the powerful a comparison with the lowly is felt to be almost unrespectable. It must therefore be avoided."[2]

Yet, from a biblical perspective, the most remarkable models of godliness emerge from among the lowly. This view from the bottom reveals that humility includes a submissive posture before God as well as a peacemaking posture with other people. To the extent that we can recover that view from the bottom, we can fortify our Christian witness in the world.

The world's competitive spirit is alive and well even in Christian circles. Our churches and institutions vie for the bodies and bucks of the same people. Many churches that boast of increasing numbers must admit that much of their growth is generated by churchgoers who transferred from a different congregation. Competitiveness can turn friends into adversaries and impede our ability to learn from those who model humility.

Even as I decry competition, I am quick to celebrate innovation and creativity, which are often born from humble circumstances. Consider the situation of many immigrants to the United States or certainly that of the descendants of enslaved Africans. Our humble circumstances are not enviable, but through adversity we turned scraps into soul food, created unique musical

[1]For a discussion of status in the ancient world, see Joseph H. Hellerman, *Embracing Shared Ministry: Power and Status in the Early Church and Why It Matters Today* (Grand Rapids, MI: Kregel, 2013). For an exploration of status in the modern world, see Isabel Wilkerson, *Caste: The Origins of Our Discontents* (New York: Random House, 2020).

[2]Klaus Wengst, *Humility: Solidarity of the Humiliated; The Transformation of an Attitude and Its Social Relevance in Graeco-Roman, Old Testament-Jewish, and Early Christian Tradition*, trans. John Bowden (Philadelphia: Fortress, 1988), 7.

forms, and developed networks for mutual support. Humility fosters collaboration, which can energize us to find solutions to problems.

I realize that our country's economic system depends on competition, and some will consider me naive to suggest that Christians think differently about our way of life. But considering how fragmented we are, how stratified our society continues to be, and how self-righteous and judgmental much of Christianity has become, perhaps increasing numbers of Jesus followers as well as Christian organizations will be open to the humble way. The way of humility leads us to transcend and even transform the oppressive elements within our competitive society, presenting faith in Jesus as leading to a radical way of life that enacts God's intentions for humanity.

Biblical humility's trajectory begins with submission to God and moves outward to embodiment, encompassing a way of thinking that undergirds community-sustaining actions.[3] Humility has an individual as well as a corporate component, starting as the proper posture we each must have before God and also supporting our relationships with others. Furthermore, humility characterizes authentic worship performed by God's people and is evidence that love is active within the community of believers.[4] Before exploring how humility relates to the way humans interact with each other, it is important to grasp how Scripture describes humility as the proper posture people must have before God. Tracing humility's trajectory from yielding to God to striving to make peace with others entails following a pathway from the Old Testament into the New Testament.

---

[3]On the concept of "way of thinking," see Eve-Marie Becker, *Paul on Humility*, trans. Wayne Coppins, Baylor–Mohr Siebeck Studies in Early Christianity (Waco, TX: Baylor University Press, 2020).

[4]Becker, *Paul on Humility*, 112.

There is some debate concerning the extent to which the Old Testament treats humility as a virtue focused on human interactions.[5] It is clearer, however, that the Old Testament offers humility as a fundamental basis for relating to God. Submissiveness to God's person and God's plans characterizes the way humble people think and act. Attitudes and behaviors that deny God's character oppose humility. Rejecting God's holiness, power, goodness—or any other divine attribute—betrays a lack of humility. Scripture abounds with examples of individuals, groups, and nations who rejected God in some way or another, failing to embrace humility. The people of Israel are no exception.

Israel struggled to practice humility in the wilderness under the leadership of Moses. With the events recorded in Numbers 11–12, we begin to trace the trajectory of biblical humility.

Humble Moses

As if carried on eagles' wings, the people of Israel were propelled to freedom from their enslavement in Egypt (Ex 19:4). Through direct action—"with an outstretched arm and with mighty acts of judgment" (Ex 6:6)—YHWH, the God of Abraham, Isaac, and Jacob, delivered the people of Israel, proving to be more powerful than Egypt's Pharaoh, army, and deities. But even after miraculous deliverance, Israel's journey through the wilderness on the way to the Promised Land proved long and arduous. Fatigue, fear, doubt, and discouragement were constant companions to the weary travelers, and their

[5]See the response of John P. Dickson and Brian S. Rosner, "Humility as a Social Virtue in the Hebrew Bible?," *Vetus Testamentum* 54, no. 4 (2004): 459-79, to Stephen B. Dawes, "Humility: Whence This Strange Notion?," *Expository Times* 103 (1991): 72-75, and Dawes, "'Ănāwâ in Translation and Tradition," *Vetus Testamentum* 41, no. 1 (January 1991): 38-48. These authors, with differing perspectives, join in opposition to the thesis of Wengst, *Humility*. The apostle Paul made humility a Christian virtue, but there is less certainty that humility expressed in interpersonal terms was considered a virtue in early Judaism.

mettle was repeatedly tested. Consequently, on several occasions, members of God's "holy nation" (Ex 19:6) became overwhelmed by their circumstances.

With their faith frequently fading, the children of Israel complained against God and God's appointed leader, Moses. The complaints of the people reveal a basic mistrust of God, or at least of God's goodness. During those times of discontent, Israel's posture toward God was adversarial, not humble. Humility, the Scriptures show, involves a submissive attitude toward God.

Numbers 11–12 records particular episodes of discontent among the people of Israel. The contrast between the complainers' behavior and that of Moses provides insights into aspects of humility. Some of the sojourners, tired of the mysterious manna that appeared six days per week (with a double portion before Sabbath), yearned for Egypt's dietary delights (Num 11:4-6). Apparently, hunger blunted memories of slavery. Craving Egypt, however, was tantamount to rejecting YHWH. The issue is not that people expressed their discomfort. Discomfort, disappointment, and pain are often expressed in the laments of Scripture. Those laments serve as examples for us of expressing the emotional pain of loss while maintaining a humble posture before God. God hears when people cry out. The problem is not lamenting life's circumstances. The problem is rejecting God. People in Numbers 11 viewed God as insufficient, or perhaps even worse, as hostile toward them. Members of the nation blamed God and looked back to their oppressors rather than embracing a posture of submission.

In response to the people's cries for meat, God sent bevies of quail—so much quail, in fact, that the complainers got sick of it (Num 11:18-20). Some Israelites died while gorging on quail (Num 11:33-34). Consequently, the location was given the name "Graves of Craving." Rejecting God demonstrates lack of humility. Israel's pining for imagined better days under Egyptian enslavement demonstrated hubris because the complainers acted as if they knew more than God knows or cared more than God cares. Despite the deaths due to arrogance, complaints continued.

Following this account, Numbers 12 opens with Miriam and Aaron, the siblings of Moses, raising a grievance against their brother. It's possible that xenophobia is lurking behind Miriam and Aaron's agitation over Moses marrying a Cushite woman.[6] The new wife of Moses is dark-skinned and from outside the Israelite people.[7] We are not given any specifics about Moses' new wife that were problematic for Miriam and Aaron, but we are privy to their complaint, in which they deny God's wisdom. They suggest that God plays favorites, saying, "Has the Lord spoken only through Moses? Has he not spoken through us also?" And the Lord hears it (Num 12:2).

It does not take long to see that Miriam and Aaron had crossed a line. God moves decisively to clarify the unique role that Moses had been given (Num 12:4-16). God appears to the three siblings in a cloudy pillar and calls Aaron and Miriam front and center.[8] Ordinary prophets, God says, get divine revelations through visions and dreams, or perhaps through obscure sayings. Yet God speaks with Moses literally "mouth-to-mouth." In light of the special relationship Moses had with YHWH, Aaron and Miriam should have thought more soberly before complaining against Moses out of fear of provoking God's anger. But now that anger is kindled.

---

[6]Cushite indicates Nubian or Ethiopian. Targum Onkelos has "beautiful" in place of "Cushite." The *Jewish Study Bible* asserts that dark-skinned women were considered beautiful. See Adele Berlin, Marc Zvi Brettler, Michael Fishbane, eds., *The Jewish Study Bible* (New York: Oxford University Press, 2004). That assessment of Africans as beautiful eventually changes as European-based Christianity develops a negative view of dark skin. See Gay L. Byron, *Symbolic Blackness and Ethnic Difference in Early Christian Literature* (London: Routledge, 2002).

[7]Most scholars agree that the unnamed Cushite wife is not Zipporah, who married Moses years earlier before the exodus from Egypt (Ex 2:21).

[8]For God's presence in the pillar of cloud, see Ex 13:21, 22; 14:19; 33:9, 10.

God inflicts Miriam with a disease that makes her skin turn white as snow.[9] Miriam's punishment is ironic; her whiteness provides a stark contrast to the skin of Moses' new wife. If Miriam has a problem with black skin, perhaps her stark white skin will teach her a lesson about judging based on skin color. Aaron beseeches Moses for mercy, who in turn beseeches God for mercy. Moses, who has been silent thus far, intercedes for his sister with a brief prayer that she be healed. Miriam is spared but must be banished from the camp for seven days. Her punishment is likened to being spit on the face by her father, an act meant to humiliate.[10]

The contrast between Moses and the complainers in Numbers 11–12 helps to clarify aspects of humility. A parenthetical observation appears in Numbers 12:3: "Now the man Moses was very humble, more so than anyone else on the face of the earth." This indicates that humility is one subject found within the curriculum of Israel's wilderness academy. This terse parenthetical description of Moses points to the starting point of humility's trajectory: biblical humility begins as submission to God.

Humility Is Yielding to God

In Numbers 11, Moses speaks a few times with people (implied in Num 11:18-20 but directly in Num 11:24, 29), but mostly with God. He prays to abate the fire of God (Num 11:2). Moses unburdens his weary soul in conversation with God (Num 11:11-15) and expresses his incredulity over God's plan to provide meat for over six hundred thousand people (Num 11:21-22). Similarly, in the

---

[9]Speculation abounds as to why Miriam is visibly punished and Aaron is not. Numbers 12:11 might suggest he expects to be punished. Because in Num 12:1 Miriam is mentioned first and the verb "spoke against" (*tedabber*) is feminine and singular, scholars suggest that Miriam instigated the accusations. Aaron may have been persuaded to make an evil choice, as appears to have been the case with the golden calf incident (Ex 32:1-2).

[10]Cf. Deut 25:9. Spitting in the face is well-known as a sign of shame in the ancient Near East, but there is no clear precedent in the Old Testament that links the shame of being spat on with banishment (see Berlin, *Jewish Study Bible*, 309).

incident with Miriam and Aaron recorded in Numbers 12:1-16, the voice of Moses is evident only in his brief prayer of intercession for Miriam (Num 12:13). The humility of Moses (Num 12:3) is primarily about his relationship with God and not as much about his posture toward others.

However, commentators typically interpret the representation of Moses as "humble" or "lowly" (*ʿanaw*) as primarily describing his gentleness or meekness in relationship with others.[11] Stephen Dawes goes as far as to assert that Numbers 12:3 is a counter to an "accusation of arrogance on Moses's part made in v. 2."[12] Yet Miriam and Aaron never actually accuse Moses of arrogance—at least not that we can see explicitly. We only get details of their complaint directed toward God. The Numbers 12 context pictures Miriam and Aaron as complaining about Moses' role as God's spokes-person. As John Dickson and Brian Rosner point out, "The thing being questioned by Aaron and Miriam is Moses' *status* not his ego."[13] The lowliness of Moses describes his connection to God more than his interpersonal connection with his siblings or with the rest of the people of Israel.[14] The Hebrew word *ʿanaw* carries a range of meanings (i.e., "poor," "afflicted," "humiliated," "lowly"), as does the Septuagint's *praus*, which is often translated as "meek" or "gentle." Both words at times describe the relatively lowly social position of some people when compared to others.[15] However, in Numbers 12:3 *ʿanaw* refers to Moses' unique relationship to God.

[11]E.g., Timothy R. Ashley, *The Book of Numbers*, New International Commentary on the Old Testament (Grand Rapids, MI: Eerdmans, 1993), 224; Philip J. Budd, *Numbers*, Word Biblical Commentary 5 (Waco, TX: Word, 1984), 136. The Septuagint's word used to describe Moses, *praus*, is how Jesus describes himself in Mt 11:29, indicating his submission to the Father (see chap. 2).

[12]Dawes, "Humility," 72.

[13]Dickson and Rosner, "Humility as a Social Virtue," 472 (emphasis original).

[14]See Gordon J. Wenham, *Numbers: An Introduction and Commentary*, Tyndale Old Testament Commentary (Downers Grove, IL: InterVarsity Press, 1981), 111. Wenham notes that humility in the Old Testament denotes "dependence on God."

[15]E.g., Is 11:4 has *ʿanaw* in parallel with *dallim* ("weak," "lowly"); LXX uses a form of *tapeinos* for both words. See Job 24:4, where *ʿanaw* (LXX: *praus*) refers to vulnerable people.

God's response to Miriam and Aaron (Num 12:6-8) confirms that Moses' humility corresponds to his submission to God. God explains that Moses has rare access to God's presence. Other prophets receive God's messages mediated through visions or dreams, but with Moses God speaks "mouth-to-mouth." The correlation of humility and intimacy with God is clear. Moses being "very humble, more so than anyone else on the face of the earth" (Num 12:3) means that he enjoyed greater intimacy with God than others did. Numbers 11–12, along with other places in the Pentateuch, show that Moses used his special relationship with God to lead Israel through the wilderness and to intercede for them in prayer.[16]

Even though humility starts as submission to God, it does not signify a relationship with God in isolation from others. Rather, our peacemaking actions and attitudes directed toward others flow out of our intimacy with God. As we follow this trajectory, we find we need another key biblical practice: repentance.

Humility and Repentance

Repentance requires humility, which entails a submissive posture before God. Repentance is the recognition of human frailty evident in our inability to be and do all that we should, regardless of the amount of physical and emotional striving. Penitent people acknowledge their need to yield to God by renouncing sin and orienting their life around God's person and words.

Some of the places in Scripture that demonstrate the role of humility in repentance are 2 Chronicles 7:14, Zephaniah 2:3, and James 1:21. The first passage, 2 Chronicles 7:14, is part of God's invitation to ancient Israel (2 Chron 7:12-21) that comes in response to King Solomon's prayer of dedication before the altar of

[16]Another moment of Moses' intercession is Num 14:13-19, which takes place during the pivotal incident at Kadesh when the people disregarded Joshua and Caleb's faithful report from their reconnaissance mission into Canaan.

the new temple (2 Chron 6:14-42): "If my people who are called by my name humble themselves, pray, seek my face, and turn from their wicked ways, then I will hear from heaven, and will forgive their sin and heal their land" (2 Chron 7:14). Humility is presented as praying, seeking God's face, and turning from wickedness. The Hebrew word translated "humble themselves" here describes submission before God and others (e.g., Lev 26:41; 1 Kings 21:29; 2 Chron 12:6, 7, 12; 30:11).[17] The connection between humility, repentance, and submission to God becomes even clearer a few verses later: "As for you, if you walk before me, as your father David walked, doing according to all that I have commanded you and keeping my statutes and my ordinances, then I will establish your royal throne, as I made covenant with your father David saying, 'You shall never lack a successor to rule over Israel'" (2 Chron 7:17-18). Obedience to God's commands, evidence of repentance, is what it means for the people to humble themselves (2 Chron 7:14).

Furthermore, Solomon and the people are called to prayer, which includes both repentance and intercession. Prayer demands honesty with God. Honesty in prayer increases intimacy with God, and that intimacy further nourishes humility, as we saw with Moses. Ultimately the "not my will but yours be done" prayer of Jesus (Lk 22:42) epitomizes humility's foundation of being yielded to God.

Zephaniah 2:1-3 is another place in the Old Testament that demonstrates how humility is first of all about submitting to God.[18]

Gather together, gather,
  O shameless nation,
before you are driven away

[17]Many occurrences of *kn*ʿ in the niphal conjugation are in 2 Chronicles.
[18]Dickson and Rosner, "Humility as a Social Virtue," 463-64.

like the drifting chaff,
before there comes upon you
the fierce anger of the LORD,
before there comes upon you
the day of the LORD's wrath.
Seek the LORD, all you humble of the land,
who do his commands;
seek righteousness, seek humility;
perhaps you may be hidden
on the day of the LORD's wrath.

At first glance the passage might appear to admonish those who have been marginalized as the "impoverished" or "poor" (*ʿanawim*) of the land, but closer scrutiny shows that the humble are those who seek the Lord and do his commands.[19] Since the same few biblical words can describe all manner of lowliness—for example, spatial, financial, emotional, psychological, and relational—there is frequently overlap. Humility, therefore, means recognizing that the materially poor and powerless—the lowly in the world's eyes—exemplify the posture we ought to have in God's presence.

In the New Testament, James 1:21 connects repentance and humility as preparation for receiving biblical teaching: "Therefore rid yourselves of all sordidness and rank growth of wickedness, and welcome with meekness the implanted word that has the power to save your souls." Meekness here, as with Moses in Numbers 12:3, indicates receptivity to God's word rather than describing interpersonal dynamics. In James 1:21, repentance is turning away from wickedness in order to receive godly teaching, and in Zephaniah 2:3, as well as 2 Chronicles 7:14, repentance can

[19]Julia M. O'Brien, *Nahum, Habakkuk, Zephaniah, Haggai, Zechariah, Malachi*, Abingdon Old Testament Commentary (Nashville: Abingdon, 2004), 114.

lead to restoration and not destruction. All three passages indicate that repentance and humility are intertwined.

Humility and Fear of the Lord

"The fear of the Lord" is a frequent Old Testament expression to describe devotion to God.[20] Humility as a posture of submission to God is reinforced in its connection to the fear of the Lord.[21] One stellar example is Proverbs 15:31-33:

> The ear that heeds wholesome admonition
> will lodge among the wise.
> Those who ignore instruction despise themselves,
> but those who heed admonition gain understanding.
> The fear of the Lord is instruction in wisdom,
> and humility goes before honor.

The synonymous parallelism in Proverbs 15:33 connects the fear of the Lord to humility. The earlier verses help to explain what is meant by both terms. Wisdom (Prov 15:31) and understanding (Prov 15:32) are found within those who possess a willingness to heed admonition (Prov 15:31) and not ignore instruction (Prov 15:32). The humble are those who are open to learning (Prov 15:33), and such instruction is correlative to the fear of the Lord.[22] The fear of the Lord is love and devotion directed toward God. Other people will benefit from that love

---

[20]The expression occurs dozens of times, ranging from Wisdom literature (e.g., Job 28:28; Prov 1:7, 29; 2:5; several more times in Proverbs), including Psalms (e.g., Ps 19:9; 34:11; 111:10), to prophetic literature (e.g., Is 11:2, 3; 33:6). The fear of the Lord is also a popular notion in Sirach (e.g., Sir 1:11, 12, 18; many other places). The term carries into the New Testament (e.g., Acts 9:31; 2 Cor 5:11). "Fear of God" is typically synonymous with "fear of the Lord" (e.g., Ps 36:1; Lk 18:4).

[21]See Dawes, " *ʿĂnāwâ* in Translation and Tradition," 44; Dickson and Rosner, "Humility as a Social Virtue," 468-70. Patrick W. Skehan and Alexander A. Di Lella, *The Wisdom of Ben Sira: A New Translation with Notes*, Anchor Bible 39 (New York: Doubleday, 1987), 159-60.

[22]See Dickson and Rosner, "Humility as a Social Virtue," 465; Bruce K. Waltke, *The Book of Proverbs: Chapters 15–31*, New International Commentary on the Old Testament (Grand Rapids, MI: Eerdmans, 2005), 8.

and devotion, but God is the chief focus. Such is the case with humility, as those who submit to God will bless others, but God is the ultimate object of devotion. Honor (Prov 15:33) comes from God rather than people (see Prov 18:12), which reinforces the idea that humility is fundamentally an attitude toward God.[23]

Another example is Proverbs 22:4:

> The reward for humility and fear of the LORD
> is riches and honor and life.

Scholars note the difficult syntactical relationship between humility and fear of the Lord. The terms are in apposition and could be rendered "humble fear of the LORD" or simply as synonyms (i.e., "humility, which is fear of the LORD").[24] The point, however, is that those who demonstrate deference to God are rewarded by God.

Humility is often viewed primarily as an ethical virtue that focuses on our willingness to defer to others. But it is more than that. A fuller picture of biblical humility develops when it is understood as primarily a posture of submission to God. The episodes in Numbers 11–12 demonstrate that mistrust of God and even rejection of God fuels criticism of God's methods. Humility, as shown with Moses, is the opposite of mistrust and encompasses complete devotion to God. The fear of the Lord, as seen in Proverbs, for example, can be equivalent to humility, with both describing devotion to God.

Numerous passages in the Old Testament connect humility to godly devotion, but one of the most well-known to Bible readers is Micah 6:8.

---

[23]Waltke, *Proverbs*, 8.

[24]See Dickson and Rosner, "Humility as a Social Virtue," 466.

Humility and Walking with God

Yielding to God is where humility starts. Biblical writers—prophets, poets, and apostles—summon humanity to humility and celebrate those who recognize their dependence on God. Micah 6:8 contains what some have considered a summary of all God's commands to the Jewish people in the Old Testament.[25]

> He has told you, O mortal, what is good;
> and what does the Lord require of you
> but to do justice, and to love kindness,
> and to walk humbly with your God?

In the second strophe of Micah 6:8, Micah calls Israel to three duties that the nation should already know and be embracing: (1) To do justice (*mishpat*), which is making right judgments according to God's instruction, (2) to love kindness (*hesed*), which is to embrace God's love, grace, and kindness, and (3) walk with God according to "humility" or "modesty" (*tsenea'*).

The term for humility here is rare in the Bible (only other occurrence is Prov 11:2), and its meaning is not clear. Many scholars understand the last line of the verse to mean something like walking wisely, or circumspectly, with God.[26] James Luther Mays concludes that the humility urged here in Micah 6:8 "lies not in going one's own way presumptuously, but in attending the will and way of God."[27] Matthew 23:23 may allude to Micah 6:8 in that Jesus declares that the "weightier matters of the law" consist of "justice and mercy and faith [or faithfulness]," a triad similar to Micah's, where faithfulness equates to walking humbly with God. Submission to God has practical implications for our treatment of others since justice and mercy coincide with walking humbly with God.

---

[25]See Berlin, *Jewish Study Bible*, 1215.

[26]E.g., Berlin, *Jewish Study Bible*, 1215; James Luther Mays, *Micah: A Commentary*, Old Testament Library (Philadelphia: Westminster, 1976), 142.

[27]Mays, *Micah*, 142.

Yielding in Practice

Competition demands winners and losers. Consequently, division and tension are endemic within competitive societies such as that in the United States. As Rebecca Konyndyk DeYoung observes, "Our culture is especially competitive. Because so many of those competitions are public, it is perilously easy to feel like we can't be good unless we're better than another, as judged and confirmed by an audience."[28] We are compelled to compare ourselves to friends, neighbors, and even strangers. Instagram makes us envious as influencers provoke our fear of missing out so that we wonder why our lives are not better. There may even be a tendency to use the social media posts of others as an indication of our relationship to God. If, for example, our network of friends includes Christian believers whose lives appear to be going well, we may attempt to mimic their behaviors. But of course, we can only copy what they allow us to see.

In this competitive environment, we take our guidance from those who fit the popular image of success, and we prefer "winners" in this competitive world. Even though Christians know humility is a biblical value, we are—like most people—drawn to those who project worldly success. But we learn humility from those who are truly submitted to God's service, and many of these people are often among the least impressive according to society's standards.

During most of my years at Cornell I attended a predominantly African American church that attracted many Black students. Like many students, I was fairly oblivious to the lives of most of the older attendees, but I appreciated their Sunday-morning enthusiasm and their joy whenever we students showed up.

One evening I was on campus in one of the student unions and happened to see a custodian buffing the floors. It jarred me a bit

[28]Rebecca Konyndyk DeYoung, *Vainglory: The Forgotten Vice* (Grand Rapids, MI: Eerdmans, 2014), 120.

when I noticed he was one of the most vocal deacons at my church, one who was always bolstering the preacher with "amen," "yes," and "help yourself, McClain." (The pastor was Rev. R. D. McClain, and to this day my wife and I fondly recall those "help yourself, McClain" admonitions.) I said hello to the deacon, and my mind went to my own parents, who labored in difficult jobs with the hope that my siblings and I would fare better in this society than they did.

Years later, when I was a pastor in Washington, DC, I often heard White people say, "No one is from DC." They never paid attention to the African Americans—the majority of the city's population—who were consistently in the background serving as cooks, elevator operators, custodians, and other service workers whose families had long lived in DC. I will never endorse the injustices that African Americans and immigrants faced—and continue to face—but I will always celebrate their faith and fortitude. Many, such as the deacon who worked as a custodian, are models of the Jesus way of life because they served God as best they could in an oppressive, competitive society. They have much to teach us all about humility.

Humility, according to the Scriptures, is not grounded in how well we compete in the world's game of life. As we observe from both the Old and New Testaments, humility begins with deference to God. The fear of the Lord and continual communion—walking—with God, in contrast to arrogant defiance of God, brings divine favor. Humility will affect our relationships with others, but it is fundamentally rooted in devotion to God. I describe humility as having a trajectory because it begins with submission to God (by individuals as well as groups), then advances outward to govern interactions between people. Those interactions, at the core, are meant to engender peace. Humility is a unifier—at least to the extent that members of the group recognize it as starting with submission to God. When members of Christian community submit to God, they are better able to submit to each other (Eph 5:21).

Since the Lord Jesus Christ is the ultimate practitioner of humility, the New Testament's portrayal of Jesus, particularly in the Gospels and Pauline letters, will guide our understanding of this often-misunderstood characteristic of Christian life.

Chapter Two

Embodying

The Example of Jesus

Humility is the raiment of the Godhead. The Word who became human clothed himself in it, and he spoke to us in our body. Everyone who has been clothed with humility has truly been made like Him who came down from his own exaltedness and hid the splendour of his majesty and concealed his glory with humility, lest creation be utterly consumed by the contemplation of him.

SAINT ISAAC THE SYRIAN

"PASTOR, YOU'RE THE BEST PREACHER I'VE EVER heard!" Imagine you're a pastor who received that accolade at the end of a worship service. How would you feel? How *should* you feel? Is there a proper way to handle such praise? What feelings and responses would communicate humility?

What if the person had said instead, "Pastor, you're the worst preacher I've ever heard"? Does humility factor into our potential reactions?

Quoted in Hilarion Alfeyev, *The Spiritual World of Isaac the Syrian*, Cistercian Studies 175 (Kalamazoo, MI: Cistercian Publications, 2000), 112.

Without exploring why people make such random comments to their pastors, we might observe that in our competitive society, we often absorb the complaints and evaluations of others when we don't need to. We compare how people respond to us and to others, looking for affirmation that we are getting ahead or at least keeping up. Reactions to social media posts, for example, may be an indication of the weight we give to others' opinions. Experts who study the effects of social media observe that "likes" as well as criticisms trigger physiological reactions. The post-sermon scenario is a simplistic example since that brief encounter with a parishioner could be readily handled and quickly forgotten. But we can imagine situations with much more at stake.

Humility guides our responses to affirmation or criticism. On the one hand, adulation might contribute to the development of a healthy self-image, where we grow in assurance that we possess unique talents, abilities, and insights from the Holy Spirit. Our spiritual gifts are used to minister to others, and receiving encouragement for the use of our gifts helps to refine and cultivate our service. Furthermore, assurance that our abilities are God-given can help to dull the pain of criticism because we weigh God's assessment to a greater degree than that of other people.

On the other hand, emotionally unhealthy people risk developing an insatiable appetite for the good feelings that come from the plaudits of others while rejecting the lessons that might be learned from criticism. When we try to satisfy the perpetual craving for compliments, it leads to obsessive self-centeredness. We begin to view other humans as the primary source of our happiness, which leads to manipulation and people-pleasing. We attempt to control people and situations with the hope of achieving the positive responses we desire while avoiding any negative feedback. Humility governs our ability to allow compliments to nurture our spirits rather than feed the monster of self-gratification. It also allows us to learn from criticism without letting it derail us.

It's important to recognize that self-image and sensitivity to how people treat us can be affected by factors beyond our control. For centuries women and ethnic minorities have been weighed down by the pressure of having their humanity questioned. Part of American Christianity's legacy is its dehumanization of those who do not conform to European images of godliness, beauty, and intelligence. There is a toll paid by those who have not only their character and integrity questioned but their humanity as well. The effect of effusive praise or thoughtless insult on a particularly love-starved psyche may be cumulative and have long-lasting consequences. But even we who have been downtrodden can find that humility empowers us to see beyond the thoughtlessness and even dangerous actions of the relatively powerful. We find supernatural power in our relationship with God.

Humility is about more than how we handle compliments or criticisms. But there is a connection, as witnessed in the example of Moses in the previous chapter. Our feelings and responses to the comments of others reflect our self-perception as well as our attitude toward God and others.

Humility, like love, must be something greater than merely a strategy we employ periodically if we think the situation warrants it. Being humble is not meant to be episodic but rather an abiding and ever-developing aspect of Christian life. When humility is embodied, our lives communicate a positive, proper, and affirming self-perception. Such self-perception is accurate in as much as it reflects the right attitude toward God and others. Jesus, the ultimate example of one who embodied humility, demonstrates its foundation as submission to God that also serves to build up others. To embody a virtue, such as humility, means that our actions accurately demonstrate our attitudes, making the concept consistently tangible in some physical way. Even if my physical body has limitations that yours might not have, I can still embody humility by making it a constituent part of my identity, incorporated into who I am and expressed in all facets of how I live.

Jesus, as the focal point of Scripture, illuminates and fulfills theological notions introduced or touched on in the Old Testament. In the Old Testament, Moses served as an example of humility's starting point, as he was "very humble, more so than anyone else on the face of the earth" (Num 12:3). The unprecedented humility of Moses corresponds to his relationship with God in that humility proved to be directly proportional to the degree of intimacy he had with God. Obedience to God, repeatedly demonstrated in the life of Moses, stands in stark contrast to stubbornness and faithlessness. The general population of Israelites in the wilderness, including Miriam and Aaron, failed to submit to God the way Moses did. YHWH spoke with Moses "mouth to mouth" (Num 12:8 KJV), and that intimacy is the basis for Moses' humility.

Jesus—the human who has eternal intimate fellowship with the Father and Holy Spirit—supremely embodies the humility that characterized Moses. As the Son who is completely submitted to the Father, Jesus is our best model and teacher. The words and actions of the Lord demonstrate humility's trajectory: it begins with submission to God, and when embodied it becomes indispensable for establishing and maintaining healthy communities.

Embodied humility is a disposition that reflects an accurate self-perception and seeks the well-being of others, making peacemaking its goal. Lowliness seeks solidarity with others, especially those on the margins of society. In his letters, the apostle Paul identifies humility as a Christian virtue, basing his understanding on the life of Jesus.[1] By employing the Greek term *tapeinophrosynē*, Paul elevates the concept of lowliness from that of the Greco-Roman perspective, and his understanding of the term reflects its trajectory from the Old Testament, through the Apocrypha, to its embodiment in Jesus Christ. Matthew's use of two related terms, "gentle" and "humble," makes his Gospel a helpful starting point for exploring the way Jesus embodies humility.

Jesus and Humility in Matthew's Gospel

Throughout Matthew's Gospel, Jesus communicates the value God places on lowliness, which is evident in his actions, self-description, and teaching. Jesus' statement about himself in Matthew 11:29 forms the basis for subsequent Christian treatments of humility, even outside the New Testament canon: "Take my yoke upon you, and learn from me; for I am gentle and humble in heart, and you will find rest for your souls" (Mt 11:29).[2] The Lord's invitation connects the virtuous concept of meekness or gentleness (*praus*), which the Septuagint uses to describe Moses in Numbers 12:3 LXX, with lowliness or humility (*tapeinos*). The term *tapeinos*, which can mean "low" or "poor," did not have a positive connotation in the Greco-Roman world. Becker contends that by coupling *tapeinos* with *praus*, which did have a "positive resonance" in the Greco-Roman world, Matthew places the humility of Jesus

[1]Eve-Marie Becker, *Paul on Humility*, trans. Wayne Coppins, Baylor–Mohr Siebeck Studies in Early Christianity (Waco, TX: Baylor University Press, 2020), asserts that Paul is the "inventor" of humility (e.g., p. xviii). Her claim is based on her observation that "in Phil 2.3, Paul coins a term that is not attested in Greek literature prior to him—ταπεινοφροσύνη/*tapeinophrosynē*" (1). Cf. Reinhard Feldmeier, *Power, Service, Humility: A New Testament Ethic* (Waco, TX: Baylor University Press, 2014), 61.

[2]Becker (*Paul on Humility*, 128) notes that "it is essentially this text—Matt 11.29—about the self-fashioning of Jesus that will lay the foundation for the fact that in later (cf. 1 Pet 3.13ff.), in some cases post–New Testament (cf. Ign. Eph 10.1ff.), times, the concrete attitudes and practices of gentleness and humility were understood from the standpoint of the person of Jesus (cf. also 1 Clem. 17.17)." Becker subsequently (136-38) takes a closer look at humility in 1 Clement.

"in a favorable light."[3] In Psalms 34:2 (LXX 33:3); 37:11 (LXX 36:11); 149:4, gentleness (*praus*) is a virtue that "can describe the proper attitude of the human being in relation to God."[4]

In Matthew 11:28, the Lord is pictured in solidarity with those he invites into discipleship. His call is to "all you that are weary and are carrying heavy burdens." Those people are themselves lowly, having been weighed down by religious requirements or perhaps simply the heaviness of peasant life. As Klaus Wengst declares, "Jesus' humility is shown in the way in which he enters into solidarity with the humiliated and those who have been brought low."[5] Likewise, Howard Thurman emphasizes the solidarity that Jesus has with the marginalized, those whose "backs are against the wall."[6] Black theology has long asserted that Jesus is Black because of his identification as marginalized and oppressed—characteristics associated with blackness:

> Although Jesus' ethnicity and dark-skinned complexion are certainly important aspects of Christ's blackness, to call Christ black points to more than simply ancestry or biological characteristics. Throughout black religious history, black people have believed that Christ identified with the black struggle against the tyrannies of a white racist society. To call Christ black affirms this identification.[7]

---

[3]Becker, *Paul on Humility*, 127. See Klaus Wengst, *Humility: Solidarity of the Humiliated; The Transformation of an Attitude and Its Social Relevance in Graeco-Roman, Old Testament-Jewish, and Early Christian Tradition*, trans. John Bowden (Philadelphia: Fortress, 1988), 76n43, who claims, "The juxtaposition of πραΰς and ταπεινός is impossible in Greek ethics."

[4]Becker, *Paul on Humility*, 127. See John P. Dickson and Brian S. Rosner, "Humility as a Social Virtue in the Hebrew Bible?," *Vetus Testamentum* 54, no. 4 (2004): 460.

[5]See Wengst, *Humility*, 76.

[6]Howard Thurman, *Jesus and the Disinherited* (1949; repr., Boston: Beacon, 1996), 3.

[7]Kelly Brown Douglas and Delbert Burkett, "The Black Christ," in *The Blackwell Companion to Jesus*, ed. Delbert Burkett, Blackwell Companions to Religion (Malden, MA: Wiley-Blackwell, 2011), 410. See also James Cone, *A Black Theology of Liberation*, 40th anniversary ed. (Maryknoll, NY: Orbis, 2010) and Takatso Alfred Mofokeng, *The Crucified Among the Crossbearers: Towards a Black Christology* (Kampen: Kok, 1983).

While the image of a yoke might suggest an oppressive, servile existence, like that of an ox or even an enslaved person, it instead points ironically to relief because the Lord is humble, joining in solidarity with those who have been beaten down by life's struggles. Jesus, according to Matthew 11:29, embodies humility because he does not merely *act* gently or humbly, but *is* gentle and humble. "Through 11.29 Matthew paradigmatically binds humility to the person of Jesus."[8] Humility is not something Jesus takes up or puts on but is intrinsic to his personhood.

Another Matthean commentary on Jesus' humility is Matthew 21:5, part of the so-called triumphal entry scene of Palm Sunday, which references Zechariah 9:9: "Tell the daughter of Zion, Look, your king is coming to you, humble, and mounted on a donkey, and on a colt, the foal of a donkey" (Mt 21:5). Jesus is the king predicted by Zechariah, and the Lord's humility (*praus*) is evident in his deportment. King Jesus does not resemble the stereotypical military champion, processing on a powerful stallion. For the astute reader, Matthew—the only Gospel author to quote Zechariah 9:9—also brings attention to the broader context of the prophecy, including the next verse, which emphasizes the king's peacemaking pursuits:

> He will cut off the chariot from Ephraim
> and the war horse from Jerusalem;
> and the battle bow shall be cut off,
> and he shall command peace to the nations;
> his dominion shall be from sea to sea,
> and from the River to the ends of the earth. (Zech 9:10)

Israel's king—foretold by Zechariah and fulfilled in Jesus—is a humble peacemaker.

---

[8]Becker, *Paul on Humility*, 127.

The word translated "gentle" in Matthew 11:29 also occurs in the Sermon on the Mount, shedding more light on how humility is embodied. In the Matthew 5:5 beatitude, Jesus declares, "Blessed are the meek, for they will inherit the earth." The term translated "meek" focuses on an inherent quality of the people.[9] The Beatitudes point to people, not to ethical ideals. As Scot McKnight deduces,

> Clearly these blessings of Jesus are not directed at ethical attributes, as if this is Jesus' version of Paul's fruit of the Spirit (Gal 5:22-23), nor is this a virtue list by which to measure our moral progress. Instead, these blessings are heaped on people groups who are otherwise rejected in society, which means the blessings console those whom many would consider hopeless.[10]

Meekness is a defining quality of the ones who will inherit the land, according to Matthew 5:5.

Jesus is also alluding here to Psalm 37:11, "But the meek shall inherit the land / and delight in abundant prosperity." In the Septuagint the word for "meek" in this verse is *praus* (Ps 37:11 / 36:11 LXX), which translates the Hebrew *ʿanawim* ("poor," also used in Num 12:3). The term is not restricted to the financially impoverished or those humiliated by society (which better describes the "poor in spirit" of Mt 5:3), but rather focuses on intimacy with God. Alert listeners and readers would hear in Matthew 5:5 an invitation to consider the context surrounding Psalm 37:11, where the psalmist urges trust in God despite opposition. Practically every verse leading up to the promise of Psalm 37:11 contains an admonition to maintain faithfulness toward God: Do not fret

[9]"Adjectives often stand in the place of nouns, especially when the qualities of a particular group are stressed." Daniel B. Wallace, *Greek Grammar Beyond the Basics: An Exegetical Syntax of Grammar* (Grand Rapids, MI: Zondervan, 1997), 233.

[10]Scot McKnight, *Sermon on the Mount*, Story of God Biblical Commentary 21 (Grand Rapids, MI: Zondervan, 2013), 33.

because of the wicked (Ps 37:1); trust in the Lord (Ps 37:3); take delight in the Lord (Ps 37:4); commit your way to the Lord (Ps 37:5); be still before the Lord (Ps 37:7). Derek Kidner, discussing Ps 37:11, points out that the meek are "they who choose the way of patient faith instead of self-assertion; a way fully expounded in the foregoing verses."[11] "Patient faith," as Kidner puts it, becomes the identifying feature of *the meek*. Faithfulness is the foundation of meekness, according to Psalm 37:11 and Matthew 5:5, which can also be described as submission or obedience. As with Moses in Numbers 12:3, meekness might also be characterized as intimacy with God.

In two other passages in Matthew, Matthew 18:4 and Matthew 23:12, Jesus uses words with the *tapeinos* root to teach lessons about humility. In Matthew 18:4, Jesus responds to the question, "Who is the greatest in the kingdom of heaven?" (Mt 18:1), by inviting a child to serve as the paradigm of humility. The Lord asserts, "Truly I tell you, unless you change and become like children, you will never enter the kingdom of heaven. Whoever becomes humble like this child is the greatest in the kingdom of heaven" (Mt 18:3-4). Jesus' emphasis in Matthew 18:3 on *changing* and *becoming* once again focuses not on a particular behavior, but on a way of being. The child serves as exemplar without apparently having to do or say anything, and Jesus bestows dignity to someone prone to be overlooked or minimized, once again showing that our moral exemplars are not always well-known or widely celebrated. Children did not possess societal status, being dependent on the care of others. Since humble people cannot overlook the humiliated, Jesus selects the child to serve as a model. Faithful disciples of Jesus can humbly turn to marginalized, dependent children and from their example learn to

[11]Derek Kidner, *Psalms 1–72: An Introduction and Commentary*, Tyndale Old Testament Commentary (Downers Grove, IL: InterVarsity Press, 1973), 150.

entrust themselves to the Lord rather than crave elevated status in society.

Matthew 23:12 reads, "All who exalt themselves will be humbled, and all who humble themselves will be exalted." This is an echo of Proverbs 3:34, "Toward the scorners he is scornful, / but to the humble he gives favor." Here is a principle that reverberates throughout the Bible: the way up is down because God rewards those who lower themselves (see, e.g., Ps 18:27; Jas 4:6; 1 Pet 5:5). The axiom of Matthew 23:12 appears as part of Jesus' teaching about how some religious leaders crave affirmation and demand respect although they are hypocrites.

> They do all their deeds to be seen by others; for they make their phylacteries broad and their fringes long. They love to have the place of honor at banquets and the best seats in the synagogues, and to be greeted with respect in the marketplaces, and to have people call them rabbi. But you are not to be called rabbi, for you have one teacher, and you are all students. And call no one your father on earth, for you have one Father—the one in heaven. Nor are you to be called instructors, for you have one instructor, the Messiah. The greatest among you will be your servant. All who exalt themselves will be humbled, and all who humble themselves will be exalted. (Mt 23:5-12)

Lowering, or humbling, oneself starts with yielding to God, which leads to a way of life that pursues human flourishing. A few verses later, in Matthew 23:23, Jesus further indicts hypocritical leaders for failing to attend to "weightier matters of the law"—namely, justice, mercy, and faith (or faithfulness). In chapter one I compared Matthew 23:23 to the admonition in Micah 6:8 to do justice, love mercy, and walk humbly with God. Stephen B. Dawes, in his analysis of Micah 6:8, gets at the trajectory of humility that

Matthew demonstrates in the life and teachings of Jesus: "The humble person is aware of other people and attentive to them in practical ways. He also pays attention to God, for humility is that mark of true discipleship which is seen in receptiveness towards God and in a willingness to listen quietly to him and let him direct one's way."[12]

Embodied humility, according to the example and teachings of Jesus—especially in Matthew's Gospel—conforms to the trajectory described in the previous chapter. Humility starts as intimacy with God—evident in a submissive posture of obedience—and expands to affect others who find in the humble person not weakness but an ability to communicate the welcoming and peacemaking posture of Jesus Christ.

Jesus and Humility in Philippians 2

There are seemingly countless analyses of the so-called Christ hymn of Philippians 2:6-10, but perhaps you, like me, find something fresh, invigorating, and life-affirming whenever you read it, which is why I frequently turn to the passage. My goal here is to emphasize that Philippians 2:6-10 reveals how Jesus embodies humility's trajectory. Paul's "master story," as Michael J. Gorman puts it, portrays how the principle of Proverbs 3:34 operates in the life of Jesus by celebrating his preexistence, incarnation, humiliation, and subsequent exaltation.[13]

Jesus personifies humility by four activities, according to Eve-Marie Becker: (1) renunciation of attributes, (2) change of form, (3) self-lowering, and (4) obedience.[14] In Philippians 2:8 the

---

[12]Stephen B. Dawes, "Walking Humbly: Micah 6:8 Revisited," *Scottish Journal of Theology*, vol. 41 (1988): 334.

[13]Michael J. Gorman, *Apostle of the Crucified Lord: A Theological Introduction to Paul and His Letters*, 2nd ed. (Grand Rapids, MI: Eerdmans, 2016), 125-27, 482-525. See also Wengst, *Humility*, 48-52, and Becker, *Paul on Humility*, who focuses on Phil 2 throughout most of her book.

[14]Becker, *Paul on Humility*, 66-72.

passage stresses Jesus Christ's obedience, which is the impetus for the other three activities. Because of his willing submission to God, Jesus did not exploit his status of equality with God for any personal gain. We might think of what Becker calls "renunciation of attributes" as using privilege for the sake of others. Jesus did not attempt to seize his divine prerogatives as if they were stolen loot but used his authority as the Son of God for the benefit of others.

The passage does not elaborate on the details of Jesus' life, but in describing the Lord as taking on the "form of a slave" even though he possessed the "form of God," it invites readers to consider the earthly ministry of Jesus.[15] As a miracle worker who healed the sick and exorcized demons, Jesus used his privileged position as the Son of God to care for and empower others, demonstrating that he came not to be served but to serve and give his life as a ransom to free many (Mk 10:45). Jesus Christ's power was not to broadcast divine entitlement or to provide personal comfort or gain. Instead, through obedience—voluntary self-emptying (*kenoō* in Phil 2:7) and lowering (*tapeinoō* in Phil 2:8)—Jesus communicated God's love for humanity. Self-emptying (kenosis) has at times been taken as an indication that Jesus abandoned aspects of deity (e.g., omniscience, omnipresence) in order to become human, but it is better to understand kenosis as metaphorically describing the Lord's sacrificial life and death.[16] Jesus emptied or *poured out* his life so that creation could flourish.

---

[15]For a rigorous treatment of Phil 2:5-11, its connection to Isaiah's Servant of YHWH, and the implications for humility, see Stephen T. Pardue, *The Mind of Christ: Humility and the Intellect in Early Christian Theology*, T&T Clark Studies in Systematic Theology 23 (London: Bloomsbury T&T Clark, 2013), 30-66.

[16]Michael F. Bird and Nijay K. Gupta, *Philippians*, New Cambridge Bible Commentary (New York: Cambridge University Press, 2020), 79-80; Gordon D. Fee, *Paul's Letter to the Philippians*, New International Commentary on the New Testament (Grand Rapids, MI: Eerdmans, 1995), 211; Gerald F. Hawthorne, *Philippians*, Word Biblical Commentary 43 (Waco, TX: Word, 1987) 86.

There was no time that Jesus Christ ceased being God, and in humbling himself to the point of death, the Lord communicates divine, self-sacrificial love. The paradoxical path of Jesus guides us away from embodying society's competitiveness and takes us along a trajectory of lowering ourselves before God so that we can be of godly service to others. While Paul's poetic passage emphasizes Christ's death, it also imagines a way of being that fosters unity. The only way to have united minds and mutual love, while rejecting vainglory, regarding others as better, and also respecting each other's mutual interests (Phil 2:1-5), is to embody humility like Jesus Christ did, no matter the consequences.[17] Philippians is rich in the wisdom needed to sustain healthy communities, so I will return to the letter in subsequent chapters in order to examine humility's peacemaking role in building and maintaining communal bonds.

Embodying Humility in Practice

"The way up is down" has become cliché in Christian circles, and in reciting that mantra we run the risk of viewing humility as a strategy for worldly advancement—as the means to an end goal of achieving success in our competitive society. If we understand *up* to refer primarily to popularity, financial success, social status, or some other indicator of winning society's rat race, we miss the meaning of humility. We might come to think of humility as merely a set of behaviors to put on display at strategic moments so that we create a favorable impression in others' eyes. Jesus said, "Whoever wants to be first must be last of all and servant of all" (Mk 9:35), but taking the last place and serving is not episodic; it is a way of life, as it was for the Lord (Mk 10:45). We learn to

[17]See Michael W. Austin, "Christian Humility as a Social Virtue," in *Character: New Directions from Philosophy, Psychology, and Theology*, ed. Christian B. Miller, R. Michael Furr, Angela Knobel, and William Fleeson (New York: Oxford University Press, 2015), 333-50.

embody humility through obedience to God and imitation of the Lord Jesus Christ, and there are manifold ways this learning takes place.

In the church of my childhood, there were folding chairs that needed to be straightened and arranged in rows, hymnbooks that needed to be placed on those seats, and a variety of other random tasks required as part of the preparation for our numerous worship services. When I was a boy, my father, with newfound faith, dragged my siblings and me to a little storefront church in Queens, New York, though my mother rarely attended.

My dad had a keen mind, quick with mental mathematical calculations and readily absorbing information in a variety of areas. His formal education, however, had been abruptly truncated due to World War II and his subsequent caretaking of his widowed mother. Despite his intelligence, my dad could be easily undervalued or dismissed because he was short in stature and African American.

Our church gatherings on Sunday took up nearly the entire day: Sunday school went from 9:30 a.m. to 10:45 a.m., the main worship service went from 11:00 a.m. to 2:00 p.m., afternoon services went from 4:30 p.m. to 6:00 p.m., and the day ended with an evening service that started at 8:00 p.m. and usually went for about two hours. Our family arrived early for services so often that my father was given a key, even though only deacons officially had keys and he was never designated a deacon.

I have vivid memories of my father arranging chairs, setting out hymnals, making sure the restrooms had toilet paper and towels, and attending to various tasks as others would trickle in the doors, often after the designated starting time for the service. After a service, even at times when my siblings and I were hungry, tired, and cranky, my father would not only help to clean up, he'd offer to drive home anyone who had taken public transportation to church.

Later in life, I attended or served as pastor of churches that met in nontraditional spaces, such as gymnasiums and VFW (Veterans of Foreign Wars) meeting halls. Members had to arrive hours before the gathering in order to set up various pieces of equipment ranging from chairs to musical instruments, microphones, speakers, projectors, and assorted paraphernalia for children of different ages. Then after the service, all those items needed to be dismantled, gathered, and stored—which at times meant transportation to a different site.

I've learned, through decades of ministry, that situations requiring physical labor in church can reveal what embodied humility might look like. The apostle Paul names "helping" as a spiritual gift (1 Cor 12:28 NIV), but taking the opportunity to join in ordinary or even menial work is not just for those with a spiritual gift; it communicates humility.

Assisting in setting up or taking down might seem like an insignificant matter, but I have often heard church attendees comment about whether their leaders joined in the group effort. Those onlookers interpreted their leaders' participation as evidence of their humility. Some leaders seemed to know they were being watched, so they made some perfunctory effort at folding a chair or two. I came to realize that those who embodied humility never really noticed what others were doing or if they were being watched; they simply served. We can learn to embody humility by imitating Jesus, as well as those who are also trying to follow Jesus. Over decades, often with a mental image of my father, I've grabbed a broom, folded chairs, wrapped up power cords, and drove people home, attempting to embody humility and not view it as a strategy to gain someone's favor.

According to Eve-Marie Becker, in the writings of the Apostolic Fathers, "practicing humility becomes a fundamental attitude toward life (Herm. Sim. VII.6 = 66.6), which goes hand in hand with patience in keeping the commandments of God."[18] Becker references a passage from the *Shepherd of Hermas*:

> I said to him, "Sir, be with me, and I will be able to endure any affliction." "I will be with you," he said, "and I will ask the punishing angel to afflict you more lightly. But you will be afflicted for a short time, and you will be restored again to your place. Only continue to be humble and to serve the Lord with a clean heart, with your children and your household, and walk in my commandments that I give you, and it will be possible for your repentance to be strong and pure. And if you, with your family, keep these commandments, all affliction will leave you; indeed," he said, "affliction will leave all who walk in these commandments of mine."[19]

The passage highlights my point that yielding to God, or obedience, is the foundation for embodying humility as a way of life in the footsteps of Jesus. When humility is embodied over time, and not seen as something to be turned on under certain conditions, we build, develop, and sustain healthy and united communities that communicate the countercultural and peacemaking nature of the Christian faith in a tense and competitive world.

---

[18]Becker, *Paul on Humility*, 136.

[19]*The Shepherd of Hermas* 66:6-7, in Michael W. Holmes, trans., *The Apostolic Fathers: Greek Texts and English Translations*, 2nd ed. (Grand Rapids, MI: Baker Books, 1999) 595-97.

Chapter Three

Communing

Mutual Love Instead of Self-Promotion

Our desire for God, then,
is not fundamentally acquisitive and violent
but dispossessive, self-emptying, peaceable.

JIM FODOR

I HAD A SEMINARY CLASSMATE WHO WAS A charmer, accustomed to getting what he asked for. He was the first person I heard declare a version of the well-worn axiom "It's easier to ask forgiveness than permission," but to me it sounded more nefarious than pragmatic. We both planned to work within the same denomination, starting new churches in different cities.

I've heard too many stories about how denominational leaders appeared to favor my classmate's sales pitches for financial support to mimic megachurch models in predominantly White suburbs while patronizing my efforts in densely populated Brooklyn, New York. On one occasion, when I asked denominational leaders about the different treatment, the superintendent responded, "Well, he's the exception and not the rule." Perhaps my inability to

---

Jim Fodor, "Christian Discipleship as Participative Imitation: Theological Reflections on Girardian Themes," in *Violence Renounced: René Girard, Biblical Studies, and Peacemaking*, ed. Willard M. Swartley, Studies in Peace and Scripture 4 (Telford, PA: Pandora Press, 2000), 257.

sell my efforts to leaders contributed to the different ways we were treated. It was clear that my colleague's ability to make his own rules impressed denominational leaders.

Our competitive society encourages people to make their own rules because the United States values so-called *self-made* individuals. However, elevating flatterers, charmers, and anyone else who cuts corners in order to achieve popularity, wealth, or political influence undermines humility's beneficial work. The mythology of the self-made person persists even though such a being does not exist—a multitude of factors always conspire to elevate some people while holding others down.

Churches should be countercultural communities of Christ followers who demonstrate how and why God is at work in the world. Yet churches are not exempt from the centrifugal forces of a competitive society that push people away from the community's center, which is Christ. Competition's kinetic energy pushes us away so that we crash into each other, causing friction and fractured relationships. Humility is centripetal, driving us toward Christ and toward each other, so that bonds are created through the sharing of life and resources. Such mutual love creates and sustains healthy Christian community.

My smooth-talking seminary classmate reported to mutual acquaintances that "Dennis is no church planter," and his words cut deeply as I sought to discern God's will on my return to New York City after seminary. Several years after starting a church in Brooklyn, my wife Susan and I followed God's call to the District of Columbia, where I served a church on Capitol Hill. After that I started another congregation in a different neighborhood. After over seventeen years in DC, Susan and I moved to Minneapolis, Minnesota, where I served an urban church for six years prior to becoming a full-time seminary professor. One consolation for me is that while I was ministering in Minnesota, about twenty-five years after the Brooklyn experience, a denominational president offered an apology saying, "We should have helped Dennis to get that Brooklyn church going." My wife and I devoted all of our years in church ministry to building bridges between people of different races, ethnic groups, and socioeconomic statuses, which sounds noble on some level, but naive on another level because genuine multiethnic ministry with people facing different socioeconomic realities is complex and taxing.

I have learned through urban life, pastoral ministry, marriage, and parenting that charm is indeed deceptive (see Prov 31:30), but humility—the fear of the Lord—is praiseworthy. Humility is the thread that holds people together, allowing for the communion that the Lord intends for his followers. Several Pauline passages reveal how humility rejects self-promotion, pursues unity, and provides the piece (or peace) often missing from congregations that desire to be multiethnic and socioeconomically diverse.

Rejecting Self-Promotion for the Sake of Communion

Humility is personal, but it can also be communal, which is to say that groups—including churches—can embody humility. Conversely, Christian communities can also embody arrogance and pride, fostering an atmosphere of self-promotion rather than unity. Imagine a scenario reminiscent of James 2:1-4, where you visit a congregation where everyone is bedecked in designer fashions and boasts of their wealth, formal education, occupations, social connections, and neighborhoods. The insider lingo, the exclusive communal activities, and the overall public presentation communicate a corporate ethos that values self-promotion. But self-promotion leads to division, while humility strives for unity.

Embodying humility requires identifying, denouncing, and confessing pride and vainglory—markers of self-promotion that lead to discord. As noted in the previous chapter, Paul commands that humility (*tapeinophrosynē*), which is demonstrated in the person and ministry of Jesus, operate as a unifying force for the Christians in Philippi: "Do nothing from selfish ambition or conceit, but in humility regard others as better than yourselves" (Phil 2:3). Christians in Philippi, a Roman colony and "leading city" (Acts 16:12), were pressured to seek honor through prideful self-promotion.[1] In Philippians 2:3, Paul rebukes selfish ambition (*eritheia*) and conceit or vainglory (*kenodoxia*), pleading instead for humility. *Eritheia* is self-centeredness that can lead to quarrels and factions. For example, in Galatians 5:20, *eritheia* (NRSV: "quarrels"; NIV: "selfish ambition") is among the works of the flesh that oppose the fruit of the Spirit.

Vainglory, Rebecca Konyndyk DeYoung observes, is "rooted in pride and in fear."[2] We might readily criticize pride, which is clearly contrary to humility and is consistently denounced throughout Scripture (e.g., Prov 11:2; 16:18; Is 2:11, 17; Mk 7:22; 1 Jn 2:16). But we often miss the way fear opposes humility. For example, we fear being insignificant, so we project an aura of expertise or strive to conform to conventional images of beauty. Fear of being overlooked or minimized fuels our pursuit of athletic prowess, wealth, or possessions. Fear forces us to take preemptive strikes against humiliation. Our competitive society stokes our fear of losing or missing out even if the spoils of victory are superficial and fleeting. DeYoung asserts that "the prideful desire superiority and the vainglorious desire the *show* of superiority, although these can easily be entangled in practice."[3] Humility, however, rejects the pursuit of superiority—real or imagined.

[1]Joseph H. Hellerman, *Embracing Shared Ministry: Power and Status in the Early Church and Why It Matters Today* (Grand Rapids, MI: Kregel, 2013), 81-101.

[2]Rebecca Konyndyk DeYoung, *Vainglory: The Forgotten Vice* (Grand Rapids, MI: Eerdmans, 2014), 7, 41-53.

[3]DeYoung, *Vainglory*, 8 (emphasis original).

Jesus Christ, as we've noted, is the example par excellence of embodied humility, demonstrated in the self-emptying of Philippians 2:6-11.

Our challenge is to move Paul's words from abstract admonitions for ancient Philippians to routine practices in our own times. Identifying pride and vainglory requires communal self-awareness. Leaders need to be self-aware, but so do entire communities.[4] Communities become increasingly self-aware as members make opportunities to listen to each other, especially to those who have been alienated and marginalized due to the community's selfishness, arrogance, and pride.

There was a sad, lonely woman who joined the church I served on Capitol Hill. Potential new members always met with the church's leadership in an informal setting, usually over dessert, and I recall her presence in a crop of new attendees who came to my home for one of those gatherings. Surprisingly, a few weeks later, this woman called me to say that she had decided to leave our church. I asked if she'd be willing to meet, and she was, so I requested that another church leader accompany me to hear her concerns. None of the leaders chose to come, and some exclaimed, "I don't know who she is; I couldn't pick her out of a crowd."

I went alone to a coffeeshop to meet with the young woman and heard her articulate how isolated she felt at church. It had been nearly impossible to make friends. As she spoke, my mind went to others who expressed concerns over the church's arrogance and cliquishness. By way of contrast, when a prominent couple decided to leave our congregation for a different church, the same leadership group granted them a meeting that lasted well over two hours, as the disgruntled couple aired their grievances.

[4]N. Graham Standish, *Humble Leadership: Being Radically Open to God's Guidance and Grace* (Herndon, VA: Alban Institute, 2007), 29-57, gives practical insight for leaders.

While listening might be an act of humility, to whom we listen is an indicator of our authenticity. Our choice of those who are worthy to get our attention might indicate our inflated sense of self-importance or the value we give to those with wealth or other status markers rather than our love for others. Most of those church leaders did not have time for the distressed woman, but were personally connected to the prominent, wealthy couple who received much attention. While the prospect of listening to people who have been hurt can seem daunting, listening—especially to those who might easily be overlooked—must be paramount within every community that claims to follow Jesus Christ. Listening helps to identify how pride and vainglory might be at work within the community.

In addition to identification, there must be public denunciation as well as confession of the sin of self-promotion, which causes discord. Public acknowledgment of sin is not self-flagellation but humility in action. While our nation struggles with how to apologize and make restitution for national sins committed against Native Americans, African Americans, and various immigrant groups, the Christian community should set the example in identifying, denouncing, and confessing evil. Christians are currently polarized, mirroring political divisions throughout the world. Humility is a weapon against polarization because it repudiates arrogance, pride, vainglory, and anything else that thwarts harmony.

Pursuing Unity

For the most part, Christians understand that unity is not uniformity, but we still struggle to define unity, much less achieve it. Unity at least means we are working together to love God and love our neighbors, sharing values and resources with Jesus Christ as the center of our relationships and actions. In Philippians 1:27-28, Paul writes, "Live your life in a manner worthy of the gospel of

Christ, so that, whether I come and see you or am absent and hear about you, I will know that you are standing firm in one spirit, striving side by side with one mind for the faith of the gospel, and are in no way intimidated by your opponents." The picturesque language of fighting shoulder to shoulder is reminiscent of the military phalanx, an image the Philippians surely understood. The unity Paul requests, however, is not based on hatred of a common enemy but is founded on humility (Phil 2:3), and Jesus Christ as the ultimate example (Phil 2:5-11).

Jesus Christ is more than merely a moral example, however; in him we not only discover humility but also learn to embody it together. "Let the same mind be in you that was in Christ Jesus," says Paul in Philippians 2:5. Paul's language here is spatial, as "in Christ" denotes the location "into which the believers are transposed."[5] Gorman sees the "in Christ" language of Philippians 2:5 and elsewhere as "not so much mystical as it is spatial; to live within a 'sphere' of influence."[6] To embody humility as those who live in Christ, we must rely on the Lord Jesus as our source. Furthermore, our corporate identity as believers who are all in Christ together means that instead of self-centeredness, mutuality and interdependence ought to characterize our communion. We must mind the interests of others and not merely our own (Phil 2:4) because we are bound together and situated in the same place—in Christ.

Being in the same location means that in some way our journeys as faithful disciples of Jesus Christ are intertwined. Our witness for God in the face of onlookers depends to a significant degree on our ability to sojourn together. Consider that we are linked to Christians of past generations as well as to others today, not only

---

[5]Reinhard Feldmeier, *Power, Service, Humility: A New Testament Ethic* (Waco, TX: Baylor University Press, 2014), 73.

[6]Michael J. Gorman, *Cruciformity: Paul's Narrative Spirituality of the Cross* (Grand Rapids, MI: Eerdmans, 2001), 36; see also Feldmeier, *Power, Service, Humility*, 72-74.

in all the good things they accomplished, but also in the shameful ways they abused power and privilege in the Lord's name. Humility means naming realities and owning up to sin, including anything from the past that could hamper our present ministries. Our corporate identity and common location in Christ do not deny individual responsibility, but rather enhance it.

We strive to embody humility in order to build up the entire community, especially the parts most likely to be pushed aside or ignored. "In Christ" refers to Christians' shared location, and so does the expression "body of Christ." Followers of Jesus constitute a collective—a single organism that Paul describes as a "body" (e.g., 1 Cor 12:12-31; Eph 4:1-16).[7] Even though the body's head is Jesus Christ, the various members need to coordinate their efforts in order to function healthily.

I've often heard Christians naively assert that divisive issues such as racism, sexism, and pretty much every other societal problem would be erased "if people got saved." Those Christians assume that all who declare faith in Jesus Christ immediately embrace common definitions of evil, denounce it, repent of it, and eagerly pursue unity. Obviously that is not the case. We gain understanding along the journey of Christian discipleship, eventually appreciating the scope of human effort involved in the process of maturation. We believe that God energizes us to "work out" our "salvation" (Phil 2:12). Yet, as we are empowered by the Holy Spirit, we must never ignore or minimize the individual and corporate energies required to build and sustain healthy communities.

Part of the struggle entails cultivating humility: "With all humility and gentleness, with patience, bearing with one another in

---

[7]Using the term *body* to refer to a group of people is not unique to Pauline writings. The term had political connotations in the Greco-Roman world. See Runar Thorsteinsson, *Roman Christianity and Roman Stoicism: A Comparative Study of Ancient Morality* (New York: Oxford University Press, 2010).

love, making every effort to maintain the unity of the Spirit in the bond of peace" (Eph 4:2-3). The first two items on this list are the terms with which we have become familiar: humility (*tapeinophrosynē*) and gentleness (*prautēs*).[8] These qualities work in tandem with patience and love to maintain the body's unity. As Becker concludes in her discussion of Ephesians 4:2 and Colossians 3:12, "Christian humility is therefore only understood correctly when it comes to stand alongside mercy, friendliness, gentleness, and patience."[9] Unity is not easy or automatic, but requires rigor—as "making every effort" (Eph 4:3) indicates. Love, as always, is supreme, but it is not always easily defined. Humility, along with other virtues, makes love tangible, not abstract or ethereal.

Multiethnic Ministry's Missing Peace

Multiethnic ministry remains a hot topic for Christians, especially in light of how increasing numbers of White churchgoers are growing in their awareness of and concern over racial injustice. For three decades I have been part of churches that pursue multiethnic ministry—to some degree or another. *Multiethnic* has often referred to the proximity of people rather than power shared among people. This has meant that the bulk of pastoral and congregational energy was spent on initiatives designed to get people of different backgrounds into the same place at the same time, but little—if any—energy had been devoted to the shared leadership and decision-making necessary to make churches truly multiethnic.[10] We might gaze approvingly at multicolored faces pictured on a church's website, yet not see how peace through humility is

---

[8]Recall the similar language in the description of Jesus in Mt 11:29: "I am gentle and humble in heart" (see chap. 2). Also, the language of humility in Eph 4:2 and Col 3:12 is consistent with Phil 2:3. See Eve-Marie Becker, *Paul on Humility*, trans. Wayne Coppins, Baylor–Mohr Siebeck Studies in Early Christianity (Waco, TX: Baylor University Press, 2020), 122-25.

[9]Becker, *Paul on Humility*, 125.

[10]See my discussion of evangelical attempts at racial reconciliation in *Might from the Margins: The Gospel's Power to Turn the Tables on Injustice* (Harrisonburg, PA: Herald Press, 2020), 179-81.

often missing in alleged multicultural churches. Potlucks, choir and preacher exchanges, and special Dr. Martin Luther King Jr. services sometimes manage to gather ethnically and racially different people together, but those efforts alone are not effective for creating the unity necessary for genuine fellowship.[11]

While several New Testament passages can inform our perspectives on multiethnic ministry, my focus here is on humility, and Paul's letter to the Colossians addresses the connection between humility and diversity.[12] The Christians in Colossae needed to remain devoted to Christ and not be drawn away by religious practices that denied the uniqueness of Jesus. Colossians 3:1–4:6 offers practical admonition for preserving Christian harmony and for making a positive impression on outsiders, but the passage also includes the instructions known as the "household codes."[13]

The reasons for and function of the household codes are debated by scholars, and these passages are problematic for contemporary readers.[14] Many read them with a hermeneutic of suspicion.[15] To a large extent, the commands in Colossians 3:18–4:1 directed to

[11]For a helpful resource to appreciating the power issues in multiethnic ministry, see Korie L. Edwards, *The Elusive Dream: The Power of Race in Interracial Churches*, 2nd ed. (Oxford University Press, 2021).

[12]I recognize also that Colossians—like Ephesians—is among the disputed Pauline letters. My focus, however, is on the language of humility at Col 3:12, and other terms describing Christian virtues that resonate with the undisputed letters. The theology and ethics are Pauline.

[13]See Dennis R. Edwards, "Colossians and Philemon," in *The New Testament in Color*, eds. Esau McCaulley, Janette H. Oak, Osvaldo Padilla, and Amy L. B. Peeler (Downers Grove, IL: IVP Academic, forthcoming).

[14]See Clarice J. Martin, "The *Haustafeln* (Household Codes) in African American Interpretation: 'Free Slaves' and 'Subordinate Women,'" in *Stony the Road We Trod: African American Biblical Interpretation*, ed. Cain Hope Felder (Minneapolis, MN: Fortress, 1991), 206-31. Martin's important study is helpful in pointing out how the household codes served to "reinforce the hierarchical, patriarchal ordering" of society (213). Martin also borrows from the work of Elisabeth Schüssler Fiorenza in arguing that the household codes are post-Pauline, written after 70 CE in order to quell the "disruption" caused by women and enslaved people in previously egalitarian congregations modeled after Gal 3:28 (211-13). Martin dismisses arguments that suggest that the household codes served as an apologia for the burgeoning Christian movement (210-11).

[15]See Carla Swafford Works, *The Least of These: Paul and the Marginalized* (Grand Rapids, MI: Eerdmans, 2019), 52-86.

women, children, and enslaved people concur with the status quo of the time, instructing members to obey the male head of the household.[16] However, despite the way these words have been used to humiliate and subjugate, they must be read in light of the earlier instructions of Colossians 3:1-17 that emphasize compassion, kindness, humility, meekness, and patience (Col 3:12 is similar to Eph 4:2). Those virtues do not support a Roman business-as-usual interpretation because they place expectations on the paterfamilias and not solely on those in the more vulnerable positions.[17] Carla Swafford Works points out how unusual it would have been in the Greco-Roman world to require the paterfamilias to exercise unconditional *agapē* (as opposed to the sexual desire of *erōs* or the affection of *philia*).[18] The paterfamilias needed humility to regulate his actions with those in subordinate positions. More could be explored regarding the household codes, but right now it is important to appreciate humility's function in multiethnic ministry.[19]

Colossians 3:11 is a key passage for considering multiethnic ministry: "In that renewal there is no longer Greek and Jew, circumcised and uncircumcised, barbarian, Scythian, slave and free; but Christ is all and in all!" In Colossians 3:11, the slave-free contrast joins that of the Jew-Gentile (Greek) distinction, seen in other parts of Scripture and described here as circumcised versus uncircumcised. Greeks presumed those who could not speak their language were uncultured and called them "barbarian" (*barbaros*). *Barbaros* was an onomatopoetic slur; Greeks called those

[16]E.g., Marianne Meye Thompson, *Colossians and Philemon*, Two Horizons New Testament Commentary (Grand Rapids, MI: Eerdmans, 2005), 96, observes, "The household codes are worrisome because they appear to perpetuate societal patterns that lend themselves too easily to domination and abuse."

[17]See Thompson, *Colossians and Philemon*, 93.

[18]Works, *The Least of These*, 82.

[19]While humility is necessary for the powerful, such as the paterfamilias, it is less obvious what humility meant for those in society's vulnerable roles. I'll explore this later in chap. 9. My interest at this point is to relate humility to the diversity of multiethnic ministry.

non-Greek speakers babblers ("bar-bar-bar"). Greeks designated Scythians—people from the region of the Black Sea, north of the Lycus Valley—as savages.[20] For Paul, when it came to ethnic, gender, and social differences, the church was to function more equitably than the broader Roman society.[21]

Harry Maier argues that while Colossae and nearby Hierapolis were ethnically diverse, Colossae attempted to assimilate the diverse cultures and the letter to the Colossians "presents a model of civic integration" that is different from "imperial acculturation."[22] Maier assesses Colossians 3:11, which expressly addresses the diversity akin to our multiethnic efforts:

> The utopian declaration of Col 3.11, that includes barbarians and Scythians, is a powerful geopolitical representation of the universal reach of Christ's rule and its power in turning enemies into friends. . . . The Roman imperial iconographic treatment of barbarians was to represent them in postures of submission or defeat. Colossians places an alternative cosmopolitan vision before its listeners' eyes. It portrays a unity of humankind brought about through the crucifixion of Jesus, a victorious death that triumphs over those "estranged and once hostile in mind," no longer enslaved to the now subjugated principalities and powers, and now joined them together in love and perfect harmony, and governed with peace (1.21; 3.13-15).[23]

Our society today, like Roman imperial iconography, treats *others* as threats that need to be vanquished or competition that

---

[20]Col 3:11 is reminiscent of Gal 3:28, but lacks the male-female contrast. For possible reasons, see Petr Pokorný, *Colossians: A Commentary* (Peabody, MA: Hendrickson, 1991), 170; Harry O. Maier, *Picturing Paul in Empire: Imperial Image, Text and Persuasion in Colossians, Ephesians and the Pastoral Epistles* (London: Bloomsbury, 2013), 94.

[21]See Scot McKnight, *A Fellowship of Differents: Showing the World God's Design for Life Together* (Grand Rapids, MI: Zondervan, 2015).

[22]Maier, *Picturing Paul in Empire*, 92-93.

[23]Maier, *Picturing Paul in Empire*, 90.

needs to be defeated. Yet Christ is the ultimate victor over evil; consequently, we join him in fighting against the forces of evil and not against each other (Eph 6:12). Even though race is a social construct developed more recently than the writings of the New Testament, we can still borrow from the lessons of Colossians 3:11 (and Gal 3:28) to heal divisions in our times.

Considering the hierarchical assumptions embedded in the Greco-Roman world, we can only imagine how the first Colossian hearers of the letter reacted to the egalitarian assertion of Colossians 3:11. It may have upset some who were comfortable with the notion of social ranking while gladdening the hearts of those yearning for respect. Since the ideals of Colossians 3:11 contradict Roman competition and hierarchy and imagine an egalitarian community, it makes perfect sense that the call for humility immediately follows: "As God's chosen ones, holy and beloved, clothe yourselves with compassion, kindness, humility, meekness, and patience" (Col 3:12). The virtues of Colossians 3:12 are necessary resources for egalitarian communities.

Our location, in Christ, means love, not social status, governs our relationships (Col 3:14). Our multiethnic congregations cannot tolerate self-promotion and status-seeking. These congregations must also reject the pride of claiming to be more multiethnic than some other congregation. Status is not the issue; love is. Humility means that multiethnic ministry is not about quotas but about peacemaking: "Let the peace of Christ rule in your hearts, to which indeed you were called in the one body" (Col 3:15). Peacemaking requires more than getting different people in proximity to each other—even though that is a start. A truly peaceful communion recognizes God-given human equality and requires those in more powerful or higher societal positions to learn from and defer to those of lower status.

It is rare to find White Christians following leaders who are Black, Indigenous, or other people of color. White people—even Christians—have gotten agitated when people of color get together to address their unique concerns. I have noticed that in some organizations, when people of color seek to start a group to support each other as minoritized people, Whites want to infiltrate in the name of *unity*. The presumed goal of White infiltration is the creation of an alleged mosaic of many colors, but in actuality the non-White members of the group get *bleached*, and the dominant culture either manages the group or patronizes it. Perhaps a better posture for White members would be respecting the need for minoritized people to caucus apart from White eyes, then humbly receiving their concerns, hopes, and recommendations.

Communing in Practice

My rejection of self-promotion does not mean denying God-given abilities, minimizing accomplishments, or refusing to strive for excellence. Rather, I intend for us to examine why we find it so important to prove ourselves to be better than others. The *participation trophy* has become a joke, especially among some parents who want their children to stand out and coaches who strive to develop exceptional athletes. Our society places an emphasis on winning, as exemplified in the adage associated with legendary football coach Vince Lombardi: "Winning isn't everything; it's the only thing." Lombardi may not have been the originator of the saying, but it speaks to the nature of competition in the sports arena and beyond.

For example, whenever there is a gathering for pastors, some feel a pressure to report ever-increasing attendance numbers or new construction as evidence of success—or winning—in ministry. Church attendees are consumers and will often leave a congregation for a different one with better programming or facilities.

For those churches who lose members, ministry can feel like a competition they are losing. Perhaps we can shift our emphases and conversations to stories of transformations in people's lives or practices we've found helpful for our own maturation in the faith.

Winning is important, certainly, but in the Christian race we run together, not against one another. Winning the Christian race means running faithfully and with perseverance (Phil 3:12-14; Heb 12:1). Perhaps because I'm part of an ethnic minority group and also an introvert, I've appreciated awards for showing up because it is easy to overlook people—especially those facing obstacles that make participation nearly impossible.

Some people have teased me about the medal for perfect attendance that I received at my junior high school graduation. Each morning over the course of three school years, I had to ride two public buses, traveling for about an hour to school while most of my classmates could start later because they walked, rode their bicycles, or got rides from their parents. The hour-long return home meant I had less time for after-school activities than most of my classmates. I suspect that some would say I *won* at attendance, but to me the award communicated that my presence mattered—that my participation was valued—even if I wasn't the valedictorian.

Humility shifts my focus away from clamoring for personal accolades as if they signify my worth to God and others. Self-promotion may not thwart all communion between Christians, or prevent the building of meaningful relationships, but we need to be careful not to focus on self-serving connections meant to enhance our status in some way. Many of us do not give our time to people who cannot help us get ahead at work, in our neighborhoods, or even in our churches. Humility contradicts such utilitarian connections, pushing us to develop sibling bonds with all sorts of people, especially those who desire to be in Christ (Gal 6:10).

Many of my ideas and interactions as a pastor failed to yield the fruit I had hoped. In fact, depending on the day, it is much easier to recall my many failures rather than what might be viewed as successes. But from my experiences as a high school math and science teacher, pastor, and college and seminary instructor, I discovered that helping people feel that they *belong* is something God has enabled me to do well. Whether it is a student struggling in the classroom, a church attendee who seems alone even in a crowd, or a stranger who appears lost, I want to see them as Jesus does—as people whose participation in life matters. I fall short, but the more I strive to embody humility, the better I get at helping others know that they matter to God, matter to me, and will matter to increasing numbers of people as they continue through life.

Relationships are rewarding in so many ways—spiritually, emotionally, pragmatically—but they are also difficult in those same ways. Humility works to create community, to develop relationships—even with people ethnically and socially different from ourselves. And it enables us to sustain those relationships when they face inevitable conflict.

Chapter Four

Reconciling

Navigating Conflict

Humility guards against jealousy, arrogance, territoriality, and rigidity. It requires that we approach contexts with care and respect; that we watch and listen to those on the margins; and that we assume that they always have something to teach us (even those of us who also live on the margins!).

CHANEQUA WALKER-BARNES

SHORTLY AFTER GRADUATING FROM SEMINARY, I returned to Brooklyn, New York, with my wife and three small children (with a fourth in utero) with plans to start a new, multi-ethnic congregation. During one of the midweek gatherings of our newly formed congregation, a young man entered who seemed more childlike than his adult body indicated. Tommy (not his real name), who appeared to be in his early to midtwenties, traveled independently, yet spoke in a singsong lilt and shuffled his feet like a toddler, never participating in our discussions.

Chanequa Walker-Barnes, *I Bring the Voices of My People: A Womanist Vision for Racial Reconciliation*, Prophetic Christianity (Grand Rapids, MI: Eerdmans, 2019), 226.

Each week Tommy returned and, by his own admission, waited for the snacks at the end of the meeting. During the end-of-meeting conversations, Tommy delighted in amazing us with his ability to name the day of the week associated with any date. Tommy once surprised me as I was riding the subway and heard his voice call out from a distance, "Pastor Edwards!" I turned and saw Tommy coming toward me from the other end of the subway car, and as he walked he exclaimed, "You were born on a Tuesday." Tommy had recalled my birthday and calculated the day of my birth, as he could do for anyone.

Our young church held congregational meetings once each quarter on a Wednesday, in place of our usual prayer and Bible study. During one of the congregational meetings, two church members voiced some disappointment over an issue. I spoke to address the concerns, as did a few others, but tensions mounted quickly and unexpectedly. We were unfamiliar with conflict in our young church, and the entire group fell silent. Tension began to fill the room. Heads drooped, as did my enthusiasm.

Suddenly, seemingly out of nowhere, Tommy's lilting voice broke the silence with, "Well, you can't please everybody!" Nearly everyone erupted in laughter. Tommy, who consistently appeared oblivious to our discussions as he waited for the snacks to be served, was God's voice in our gathering. A prophetic pronouncement came from someone lowly in the eyes of the world—including the eyes of church members in our young fellowship.

We needed to learn that conflict is part of the human experience. No matter how lofty our goals might be, how well-scripted our values, and how well-intentioned our acts, there will inevitably be conflict. We can't please everybody all of the time. Genuine community reflects the character of God, but it is always under threat, despite our best attempts to foster solidarity. Conflicts are unavoidable and some unresolvable, but they can be negotiated. Negotiating conflict means pursuing the way of peace, which requires that humility govern our interactions.

The components needed for building a house, such as lumber, cement, and metal, are also the materials used for repairs. Similarly, humility is a key trait needed for both establishing and maintaining Christian community. Most relationships typically start with enough good intentions and mutual submission to move beyond a casual encounter to something more substantial. It is inevitable, however, that conflicts will emerge. This happens for any number of reasons, and some of our hostility stems from differing theological perspectives, status in society (including race, gender, and economics), and a range of interpersonal differences that might foster factionalism and provoke division. I hasten to point out that some theological differences are obvious in their distortion of the character of God and may be considered evil. Such is the case in Jude 4, for instance, where Jude denounces interlopers "who pervert the grace of our God into licentiousness and deny our only Master and Lord, Jesus Christ." Humility helps to discern what Scripture categorizes as evil. Since humility starts with yielding to God and propels us to peacemaking, it enables us to be attentive to the voice of God in Scripture and also to what distorts the image of God in the world. Consider patriarchy, for example. Humility pushes us to see how some readings of biblical passages have contributed to the oppression of women because humility opens my eyes not only to the words on the pages but also to the way those words are interpreted and applied. Humility allows me to discern oppression even if I'm not the direct recipient of that oppression.

It would be naive to suggest that conflicts can be resolved simply, or that they all can be resolved. However, following the way of Jesus includes "making every effort to maintain the unity of the Spirit in the bond of peace" (Eph 4:3). The Spirit of God compels us to resolve conflict, and humility is a lubricant that decreases friction, allowing sets of dug-in heels to slide closer to opposing sets of heels. Perhaps humility can salvage relationships, reducing the number of divorces, fractured friendships, and church splits. With humility we get off the treadmill of trying to please everyone and redirect our energies toward following the pathway of Jesus.

The Jesus path, however, is radical. The countercultural path of humility follows a trajectory of submission to God along with an orientation toward those of lower status—the people who are in a comparatively more vulnerable position. When humility is embodied as a way of life, we can embrace conflict, navigate it, and resolve it in ways that honor God and strengthen human bonds. Several passages in Pauline writings help us to imagine how humility can address a range of conflicts found within Christian communities. Some New Testament readers (including some of my students) find the apostle Paul to be arrogant, aggressive, and not at all humble, so it is ironic that he is the one who has much to teach us about humility. While I do not suggest that Paul always mirrors in his actions the virtues that he admonishes in his writings, I will say that humility does not mean a lack of assertiveness or a rejection of firm truth-telling. Jesus, for example, pronounces "woe" to religious leaders (e.g., Mt 23:13-32) in the same Gospel where he is described as gentle and humble (Mt 11:29).

Galatian Subjugation

In Galatians, it seems that Paul addresses problems associated with Torah-observant Jewish followers of Jesus expecting Gentile converts to observe the Torah—or at least aspects of it—on their conversion. Paul would not have Gentile followers of Jesus pressured into circumcision and dietary restrictions, and neither would he have his apostolic authority undermined. Requiring followers of

Jesus to submit to the Torah's demands amounts to a different gospel, according to Paul, one that he had not been preaching (Gal 1:6-9). What the Galatians were learning from Paul's opponents was a perversion of the gospel of Christ. In Galatians 5–6 Paul wraps up his argument by offering a formula for community health. Humility is central to Paul's pastoral admonitions.

For Paul, if Christians submit to the "yoke" of Torah as a requirement for following Jesus, they distort the gospel and subvert their freedom found in Christ (Gal 5:1). We contemporary readers rightly spend energy trying to understand Paul's theological concerns in Galatians, especially since his opposition is unnamed.[1] However, we must not minimize the practical and pastoral imperatives that build from Paul's theological arguments. Those admonitions rely on humility as the outworking of love required to heal wounds of division and build a unifying culture among Jesus followers.

Galatians 5:13 highlights humble expressions of love that can heal division: "For you were called to freedom, brothers and sisters; only do not use your freedom as an opportunity for self-indulgence, but through love become slaves to one another." Paul's words are radical and paradoxical. Not only are we agitated—and even offended—at the notion of enslavement, but we have seen Paul denounce the "yoke of slavery" a few verses earlier in Galatians 5:1.[2] In fact, Paul has stressed liberation throughout the entire letter.[3]

---

[1]E.g., John M. G. Barclay, "Mirror-Reading a Polemical Letter: Galatians as a Test Case," in *The Galatians Debate: Contemporary Issues in Rhetorical and Historical Interpretation*, ed. Mark D. Nanos (Peabody, MA: Hendrickson, 2002), 367-82. Cf. Craig S. Keener, *Galatians: A Commentary* (Grand Rapids, MI: Baker Academic, 2018), 31-36.

[2]James D. G. Dunn, *The Epistle to the Galatians*, Black's New Testament Commentary (1993; repr., Grand Rapids, MI: Baker Academic, 2011), 289, comments on *douleuō*, asserting, "The use of the verb, literally, 'to perform the duties of a slave,' would be intended to have some shock effect, since in Greek thought slavery was the complete antithesis of freedom."

[3]See Keener, *Galatians*, 483; Reinhard Feldmeier, *Power, Service, Humility: A New Testament Ethic* (Waco, TX: Baylor University Press, 2014), 35-39.

Rather than use the verb *diakoneō*, which refers to a range of service, including waiting on tables and assorted church duties, in Galatians 5:13 Paul uses *douleuō*, a word that describes subservience, translated "become slaves." But in doing so he is not calling for giving up one's human autonomy; rather, he's referring to what is necessary for thriving relationships.[4] Also, in using *douleuō* rather than *diakoneō*, Paul seems to be deliberately alluding to his use of the militaristic verb *katadouloō* (enslave) in Galatians 2:4: "False brothers and sisters . . . slipped in to spy on the freedom we have in Christ Jesus, so that they might enslave us" (NRSVUE). The idea is that rather than being enslaved by false Christian siblings, the Galatians are to give themselves in service to their true sisters and brothers.

Galatians 5:13 communicates the revolutionary nature of humility. Serving one another counters the biting and devouring characteristic of conflict (Gal 5:15). The first part of Galatians 5:13 stresses that the goal of Christian liberty is not to satisfy personal (*fleshly*) desires, and thereby emphasizes humility. Humility is a mindset that favors solidarity (see chapter three) and depends on selfless actions born from love. Therefore, the enslavement Paul advocates cannot mirror the oppressive institution of slavery endemic throughout the Roman Empire.

Ironically, enslaved people can provide the model for virtuous Christian discipleship (e.g., 1 Pet 2:18-25). The apostle Paul, immersed in the slave society of the Roman Empire, declares, "I have made myself a slave to all" (1 Cor 9:19), and describes himself as slave of the Master, the Lord Jesus Christ (e.g., Rom 1:1; Gal 1:10).[5] Christ's service to humanity is described

---

[4]See Feldmeier, *Power, Service, Humility*, 35.

[5]See Dennis R. Edwards, "Slave, Slavery," in *Dictionary of Paul and His Letters*, 2nd ed., ed. Scot McKnight, Lynn H. Cohick, and Nijay K. Gupta (Downers Grove, IL: IVP Academic, 2023), 994, for a discussion of Paul's use of slave imagery to describe his ministry. Also, John Byron, *Recent Research on Paul and Slavery*, Recent Research in Biblical Studies 3 (Sheffield: Sheffield

as enslavement in Philippians 2:7-8. Jesus took on the form of a slave and is the quintessential example of humility. Enslavement to Christian siblings, based on supernatural love, describes a bond unlike that found in the rest of society because it rejects hierarchies and status-seeking.

Earlier in the letter, Paul puts forward his liberating Jesus-centered ethic for Christian community: "There is no longer Jew or Greek, there is no longer slave or free, there is no longer male and female; for all of you are one in Christ Jesus" (Gal 3:28). This oneness is based on union with the Lord Jesus Christ and transcends society's boundaries of ethnicity, social status, and sex. While Jew/Greek, slave/free, male/female boundaries exist outside the Christian community, they do not carry the same significance for Christians. The energy required to enforce the boundaries is stripped away and replaced by the power of the Holy Spirit, who creates equity in relationships.

Paul's vocabulary for humility in Galatians is different from that in Philippians, but he touches on similar ideas in his list of the Holy Spirit's fruit (Gal 5:22-23). The entire list is worthy of reflection, but it is *prautēs*, the word translated "gentleness" in Galatians 5:23, that connects most clearly to the New Testament's picture of humility. *Prautēs* is related to *praus* (see chapter one), describing temperance, and was viewed favorably in the Greco-Roman world.[6] Both *prautēs* and *praus* are connected to lowliness (*tapeinophrosynē* and cognates) in the New Testament, as we've seen in previous chapters.

Phoenix Press, 2008), 67-91, and Mitzi Smith, "Slavery," in *True to Our Native Land: An African-American New Testament Commentary*, ed. Brian K. Blount et al. (Minneapolis, MN: Fortress, 2007), 11-22.

[6]Eve-Marie Becker, *Paul on Humility*, trans. Wayne Coppins, Baylor–Mohr Siebeck Studies in Early Christianity (Waco, TX: Baylor University Press, 2020), 127.

Table 4.1. Humility in Matthew 11:29, Ephesians 4:2, and Colossians 3:12

Matthew 11:29	Take my yoke upon you, and learn from me; for I am gentle [*praus*] and humble [*tapeinos*] in heart, and you will find rest for your souls.
Ephesians 4:2	with all humility [*tapeinophrosynēs*] and gentleness [*prautētos*], with patience, bearing with one another in love
Colossians 3:12	As God's chosen ones, holy and beloved, clothe yourselves with compassion, kindness, humility [*tapeinophrosynēn*], meekness [*prautēta*], and patience

These three passages demonstrate that lowliness and gentleness work together. The meekness associated with *praus* is not weakness or false modesty, but a way of being that yields to God and honors other people. Galatians helps us to see that negotiating conflict entails recognizing the unity of Christians regardless of society's boundaries (Gal 3:28) along with deferential service to one another through love (Gal 5:13-14), empowered by the Holy Spirit (Gal 5:22-23). Conflicts emerge within all groups of people, even those seeking to live as subjects of King Jesus, but humility fosters harmony. People who embody humility refuse to endorse society's stratification and instead rely on the Holy Spirit, taking their cues from the lowly—enslaved people—to learn the radical nature of Christian love for one another.

Roman Wrangling

Although scholars debate the occasion for Romans, Scot McKnight provides a novel and helpful perspective in *Reading Romans Backwards: A Gospel of Peace in the Midst of Empire*, where his mirror reading of Romans leads him to conclude that "*all of Romans* must be read in light of the context of Romans 14–15."[7] According to McKnight, those whom Paul called "the weak" were Torah-observant Jews, while the predominately Gentile ("strong") Christians exercised freedom from following Torah rituals.

[7]Scot McKnight, *Reading Romans Backwards: A Gospel of Peace in the Midst of Empire* (Waco, TX: Baylor University Press, 2019), 180 (emphasis original).

Romans commentators universally acknowledge the weak/strong conflict, but McKnight breaks from the pack in suggesting that Romans 12–16 does not simply represent Paul moving from didactic material to practical guidance. For McKnight, Romans is not a "classic example of the indicative leading to the imperative. What Paul had in focus was the lack of praxis, the lack of lived theology, the lack of peace in Rome, and he wrote Romans both to urge a new kind of lived theology (12–16) and to offer a rationale (1–11) for that praxis."[8] McKnight's analysis demonstrates that concord among the Christians in Rome was central to Paul; it was not simply good advice to add near the end of his letter. Paul sought to guide Roman Christians in negotiating conflict in order for them to experience Christ's peace. Romans 12:16 highlights the centrality of humility in negotiating conflict.

The lived theology of Romans 12 includes echoes of the teachings of Jesus in the Gospels.[9] What Paul writes regarding humility in Romans 12:16 is also conceptually and linguistically similar to Philippians 2:3. In Philippians 2:3 Paul urges *tapeinophrosynē*, "humility," and he uses the two components of that word in Romans 12:16, *tapeinos* and *phroneō* (think, have in mind).[10]

Table 4.2. Humility in Romans 12:16 and Philippians 2:3

Romans 12:16	Philippians 2:3
Live in harmony with one another; do not be haughty, but associate with the lowly [*tapeinois*]; do not claim to be wiser than you are.	Do nothing from selfish ambition or conceit, but in humility [*tapeinophrosynē*] regard others as better than yourselves.

Since "the lowly" (*tapeinois*) in Romans 12:16 can grammatically be either masculine or neuter, it could refer to people or things. Thus Paul could be commanding that his readers associate

[8]McKnight, *Reading Romans Backwards*, xiv.

[9]A clear example is "Bless those who persecute you; bless and do not curse them" (Rom 12:14); cf. Lk 6:28.

[10]In fact, *phroneō* appears twice along with its cognate *phronimos* in Rom 12:16.

with people of low status, as reflected by most contemporary English translations. Or Paul's imperative might instead be urging the Romans to perform lowly tasks—work viewed as menial, not prestigious (e.g., ASV's "condescend to things that are lowly" and NRSV's marginal reading: "give yourselves to humble tasks"). The former possibility—associating with those of lower status—is the more likely option. Paul instructs the Roman Christians, as he did the Galatians, to oppose the barriers of social status. Paul expects those with privilege or rank within society to be deliberate about embracing those without prominence. As with the Christians in Galatia, relationships among the Romans must be equitable, unlike the competitive and hierarchical environment in which the believers find themselves.

In the competitive Greco-Roman world, "the counterpart of the lowly and the humble man is the high-minded man."[11] The phrase "do not be haughty" in Romans 12:16 could also be translated "do not think on high things." Paul is making a contrast between high (*hypsēlos*) and low (*tapeinos*). Klaus Wengst does well to acknowledge that the pursuit of that which is *hypsēlos* is essentially going after "wisdom gained apart from the others and with personal interests in mind, oriented 'above.' It goes with looking for promotion, the quest for upward mobility. Such wisdom and such a concern disrupt solidarity and lead to competition."[12] In order for Christians to establish harmonious relationships they must reject high-mindedness, self-promotion, and status-seeking.

To achieve concord, those with status are to associate with the lowly. "Associate" translates the rare word *synapagō*. In its two other New Testament appearances it has the negative sense of

[11]Klaus Wengst, *Humility: Solidarity of the Humiliated; The Transformation of an Attitude and Its Social Relevance in Graeco-Roman, Old Testament-Jewish, and Early Christian Tradition*, trans. John Bowden (Philadelphia: Fortress, 1988), 7.
[12]Wengst, *Humility*, 47.

being led or carried away by hypocrisy or error (Gal 2:13; 2 Pet 3:17). Perhaps Paul is being ironic in Romans 12:16 because those in privileged positions could never imagine themselves being led by those of a lower station.[13] Paul may be commanding that those who view themselves as superior to allow themselves to be "carried away" by the allegedly inferior. Resolving conflicts with humility means centering those who are in the less prestigious place. The lowly are likely to have their perspectives overlooked or outright rejected. Yet often those in the lower position actually have the better perspective of any unfair system.[14]

Humility is part of a healthy strategy for spiritual growth through conflict. Such humility involves shifting from strategies for self-promotion to attitudes and behaviors that strive for harmony, focusing on the concerns of people occupying low rank in society.

Corinthian Quarreling

The Christians in Galatia and Rome were not the only believers to receive written communication from the apostle Paul urging humility in order to heal damaged relationships. Restoring unity is Paul's expressed goal in writing 1 Corinthians.

> Now I appeal to you, brothers and sisters, by the name of our Lord Jesus Christ, that all of you be in agreement and that there be no divisions among you, but that you be united in the same mind and the same purpose. For it has been reported to me by Chloe's people that there are quarrels among

[13]Becker, *Paul on Humility*, 101-2, notes the "negative connotation" and paradoxical nature of *synapagō*. After explaining Paul's vocabulary, Becker assesses that "Paul, in 12.16, coins expressions that change—and thus turn on their heads—the self-perception and perception of others of the groups involved in the controversy."

[14]E.g., Charles W. Mills, *The Racial Contract* (Ithaca, NY: Cornell University Press, 1997), observes how "the term 'standpoint theory' is now routinely used to signify the notion that in understanding the workings of a system of oppression, a perspective from the bottom up is more likely to be accurate than one from the top down" (109).

> you, my brothers and sisters. What I mean is that each of you says, "I belong to Paul," or "I belong to Apollos," or "I belong to Cephas," or "I belong to Christ." (1 Cor 1:10-12)

Quarrels accompanied the formation of factions. In addition to the various alliances that Paul mentions, the Corinthian Christians debated what constitutes appropriate conduct, with arguments between the "weak" and "strong" (1 Cor 8:1–11:1).[15] Some members of the church marginalized other believers (1 Cor 11:17-34).

Humility is always part of the remedy required to cure division. Humility is an imperative for reconciliation, and that comes through in Paul's metaphorical use of "body" in 1 Corinthians 12. As with Galatians 5:13 and Romans 12:16, Paul describes humility's emphasis on the lowly, those most likely to be overlooked. In Galatians 5:13 enslaved people provide the model for how Christians ought to humbly serve each other. In Romans 12:16 humility means deliberate connection with and respect toward those viewed as inferior, or lower in society. In 1 Corinthians 12, Paul is explicit in commanding that the vulnerable, those perceived as "less honorable," receive greater honor:

> On the contrary, the members of the body that seem to be weaker are indispensable, and those members of the body that we think less honorable we clothe with greater honor, and our less respectable members are treated with greater respect; whereas our more respectable members do not need this. But God has so arranged the body, giving the greater honor to the inferior member, that there may be no dissension within the body, but the members may have the same care for one another. (1 Cor 12:22-25)

[15]Weak and strong are the same adjectives used to categorize the Roman Christians (e.g., Rom 14:1–15:13).

In Paul's metaphor the less honorable body parts refer to those that typically get covered in public, but the point of the comparison is to address human relationships. In the church, God requires that the community pay greater attention to the concerns, needs, and voices of those deemed to be inferior, dignifying them for who they are and not focusing primarily on the role they play in society. Paul describes the ones "that seem to be weaker" as "indispensable" (NRSV) or "necessary" (KJV).

For competitive societies, weakness is shameful, so the vulnerable are taken to be inconvenient, kept hidden, or worse. Ancient Roman society disposed of weak children, and some, retrieved from the trash heap, were enslaved.[16] In our time ableism stigmatizes people who were born with or have developed physical challenges or limitations. Michael A. Walker defines ableism as "the systemic and personal oppression of people with disabilities, in favor of people of able body."[17] Our society even tends to accept or excuse powerful bullies who seem to be able to get us something we want. Perhaps certain political figures, business leaders, and even church officials come readily to mind, but so might coworkers and family members. Through years of my athletic competitions, cheering on my children in their competitions, and teaching student-athletes, I became aware of athletically talented students (affectionately called jocks) bullying other people but not facing punishment or correction.

For God's church, however, greater honor must be given to those in the vulnerable, inferior position. Paul argues that by honoring those most likely to be dishonored, communities can avoid division. Unity through humility is possible when those in relatively powerful positions adopt the perspectives of those who have been marginalized.

---

[16]Mary Beard, *SPQR: A History of Ancient Rome* (New York: Liveright, 2015), 315.

[17]Michael A. Walker, "Persistent Pain and Promised Perfection: The Significance of an Embodied Eschatology of Disability," *Journal of Disability and Religion* (2023): 111.

Philippian Friction

The extent to which conflict polarized the Philippian Christians is not clear, yet unity is one of Paul's aims in writing the letter. Also, we know that an internal conflict between two women disturbed the apostle Paul enough for him to call out the women in front of the entire community. Paul urges Euodia and Syntyche "to be of the same mind [*to auto phronein*] in the Lord" (Phil 4:2).[18] This echoes Paul's admonition to the entire community given earlier in Philippians 2:2.[19] What is true for solidarity in the entire community must also be true on the interpersonal level. We know nothing of Euodia and Syntyche beyond what Paul writes in Philippians 4:3: that these women have "struggled beside me in the work of the gospel."[20] That description, however, is enough for us to imagine women possessing great faith and fortitude, since we know that Paul did not have a carefree life. Euodia and Syntyche have led by example and will continue to do so. Consequently, their example needs to be a positive one—they need to pull together rather than apart. Paul calls them to acknowledge their challenges, accept help, and come to an agreement instead of each asserting that her own way is best. This all would require humility.

Humility is not only required of the clashing women, it is also a feature of the unnamed party tasked with helping to heal the division. In Philippians 4:3 Paul appeals to *syzygos*, literally "yoke fellow," which is likely a descriptor rather than a proper noun. Interestingly, the one called to help may not be named, while the women who clashed are, as is another coworker, Clement, later

[18]When English versions (e.g., NLT) neglect to translate both occurrences of *parakalō* (I urge) in Phil 4:2, we risk losing the force of Paul's rhetoric in addressing his concern for each woman.

[19]See the discussion of Philippians in chap. 3.

[20]Euodia translates to "good journey" and Syntyche to "good luck." Their names suggest that they may have been enslaved at some point in their lives. See Michael F. Bird and Nijay K. Gupta, *Philippians*, New Cambridge Bible Commentary (New York: Cambridge University Press, 2020), 172.

in Philippians 4:3. Surely the Philippians knew the yoke fellow even if we do not.[21] Still, we can discern the type of person this is from Paul's description and expectations. The yoke fellow is another colaborer of Paul's, as the yoke image implies. This is a person who understands what is at stake in the service of the gospel and who would know what Euodia and Syntyche have experienced in their work with Paul. Furthermore, the yoke fellow is described as "loyal" or "genuine." That is also how Paul describes Timothy (1 Tim 1:2) and Titus (Titus 1:4).[22] The term indicates a person with a good reputation, who can be trusted to carry out what Paul asks.

The work of this *syzygos* yoke fellow is perhaps more nuanced than the NRSV's translation "help" suggests. The verb *syllambanō* is a word with a range of meanings and can describe apprehension or arrest by authorities (e.g., Mk 14:48; Acts 12:3), netting fish from a boat (e.g., Lk 5:7, 9), or the conception of a child (e.g., Lk 1:24; Jas 1:15). Every New Testament occurrence outside Philippians 4:3 evokes a tactile image where physical touch is involved or somehow engages the physical body (as in the case of Mary's conception of Jesus).[23] Such might be the case here in Philippians 4:3 as well. Euodia and Syntyche needed something other than a stern talking-to or a passive-aggressive message from the pulpit. They needed a trustworthy person to take them by the hand (perhaps literally) and sit with them to work through their differences. These two women leaders needed to be proximate in order to resolve their conflict, and a trustworthy third party, this loyal yoke fellow, was Paul's choice to make it happen.

---

[21]Epaphroditus (Phil 2:25) seems the most likely candidate for the label *syzygos* (see Bird and Gupta, *Philippians*, 173).

[22]While I realize Pauline authorship of the pastoral epistles is disputed, the undisputed Pauline letters paint a picture of Timothy and Titus as faithful proteges of Paul (e.g., 1 Cor 4:17; 2 Cor 8:23).

[23]*Syllambanō* followed by a dative (of a person) suggests assistance that is often physical. For example, *Lysistrata* (line 540) by Aristophanes; the women are told to put down their jars in order to assist their friends, and that assistance requires physical touching.

Working through conflict is strenuous activity, as implied by the other uses of *syllambanō*. The effort pays off because discord is a virus that can infect organizations. Humility fights the discord disease by degrading the ingredients that foster division and by nurturing healthy relational habits. Paul's instruction to "be of the same mind" in the context of creating harmony is similar to the modern idiom "a meeting of the minds." But for those minds to meet, there must be someone who can bring the feuding parties together. Humility allows a meeting of the minds. Humility pushes Euodia and Syntyche to meet and pull together, but they need to receive the assistance of a peacemaker. Humility is also active in the third party whose reputation validates them as the right candidate to broker reconciliation.

Reconciling in Practice

Conflict is inevitable and threatens the harmony of all relationships, including those that hold church communities together. Humility is a tool in the Holy Spirit's toolbox that repairs damaged relationships. Theological differences, even deeply entrenched ones, need not be the cause of hate and vitriol, leading to social separation.

For example, while the theological differences between Roman Catholicism and Protestantism are great and far-reaching, I've noticed in my lifetime a decrease in the hurtful rhetoric previously lobbed from each side toward the other. Perhaps that rapprochement is part of this post-Christian era's diminishing concern to draw lines of doctrinal separation. Even though some decrease in tension may simply be the result of theological ignorance, or indifference toward Christian doctrine, humility may also be at work in bringing together increasing numbers of people who claim that Jesus is Lord. In recent decades there have been meetings between some Roman Catholic and Protestant denominational leaders. More meetings are yet on the horizon. Academics have long been drawing from scholars within various ecclesial traditions. The divisions are not always as stark and hurtful as in bygone days.

However, most Christians do not feel ecclesial conflict on the larger denominational scale, but on the smaller, interpersonal, and hence more painful level. Paul's language about a way of thinking (*phronēsis* and related terms) means that we open our minds to new possibilities. Paul urges us to think in fresh ways, even when it comes to local theological differences. I have done this on a personal level as I wholeheartedly embraced the notion of women leaders in the church even though I grew up attending an emphatically patriarchal church. I also broadened my understanding of baptism. Along the way I began by appreciating people with different views even before fully understanding their practices.

This seems consistent with the way Paul presents adjustments in thinking as not primarily conformity to new ideas, but honoring *sisters and brothers* who think differently. Humility allows a fresh way of thinking that keeps relational connections at the center, as those connections are based on mutual faith in Christ. It may be that we will adopt a different course of action in our practice of the faith, but more importantly we will not lose sight of the reality that those with whom we differ are our *sisters and brothers*.

As I strive to embody humility, I learn that my Christian responsibility to sisters and brothers is deferential service, as Paul points out in Galatians 5:13. Deferential does not mean demeaning even though Paul employs the language of slavery.[24] According to R. Robert Creech,

[24]As pointed out in the introduction, the struggle not to confuse humility with humiliation is real and will always be with us.

> When a pastor knows of issues between congregants or factions in the congregation and addresses the content rather than the emotional process, the triangles can become divisive and destructive. . . . Notice Paul's firm but gentle words to two women in Philippi and to their pastor: "I urge Euodia and I urge Syntyche to be of the same mind in the Lord. Yes, and I ask you also, my loyal companion, help these women" (Phil. 4:2-3). We do not know what the dividing issue was. For Paul, the relationship mattered most. Pastors who are learning to "think systems and watch process" might find creative ways to engage such anxious relationships in the church.[25]

My pastoral service—whether or not I bear the title "pastor"—might include being a reliable peacemaker for those alienated from each other. The peacemaking role is emotional, not entirely informational, and invites us to exercise emotional intelligence along with our biblical knowledge.

I have written elsewhere about the importance of knowing that God honors people whom the relatively powerful and privileged view as weak vessels.[26] Elderly people, those who are not conventionally attractive, or not athletic, or not formally educated, or dark-skinned—the list can get quite long of those who get marginalized in our world—are considered weak by the world's standards. Yet these apparently weak people are often the best witnesses of God's strength. As the apostle Paul told the church at Corinth, "But God chose what is foolish in the world to shame the wise; God chose what is weak in the world to shame the strong" (1 Cor 1:27). Shame on us if we fail to see God at work in those we label as weak.

---

[25]Note the observation of R. Robert Creech, *Family Systems and Congregational Life: A Map for Ministry* (Grand Rapids, MI: Baker Academic, 2019), 67-68.

[26]See Dennis R. Edwards, *Might from the Margins: The Gospel's Power to Turn the Tables on Injustice* (Harrisonburg, PA: Herald Press, 2020).

When Tommy showed up to our Brooklyn church's Wednesday gatherings, some saw him as a nuisance who ate our snacks and brought nothing to share. It was not clear how he'd contribute to our fledgling ministry. But it was Tommy who sensed the conflict in our meeting that evening, and his "you can't please everybody" comment diffused the tension. Tommy brought down the emotional temperature in the room and spoke wise words we needed to hear—words that have resonated with me for decades. God speaks through those we are prone to ignore, so we must listen, especially if we are called as shepherds or leaders for any number of people.

Chapter Five

Shepherding

Setting an Example Through Service

Pride makes us artificial,
and humility makes us real.

Thomas Merton

In June of 68 CE, Servius Sulpicius Galba became emperor of Rome after the death of Nero, who had earlier entrusted Galba with a military command, assessing Galba as "too old and mild to rebel."[1] In his brief reign as emperor, Galba managed to frustrate, alienate, and infuriate soldiers as well as political leaders. According to Suetonius, Galba was cruel and greedy, as shown in his levying severe taxes on townships slow to receive him, his execution of rivals along with their families, his tendency to sentence nobility—including senators—to death without trial or with only slight evidence, and his reluctance to approve applications for Roman citizenship.[2]

Galba had no children of his own and selected an heir that no Roman leader or soldier approved of. The named successor, Lucius Calpurnius Piso Licianianus, had no military experience and had

---

Thomas Merton, *No Man Is an Island* (Boston: Shambhala, 2005), 119.

[1]Michael Grant, *The Twelve Caesars* (New York: Scribner, 1975), 179.

[2]Suetonius, *The Twelve Caesars*, trans. Robert Graves, Penguin Classics (New York: Penguin, 2003), 256-57.

relatives who opposed Nero, whom the military generally respected.[3] The soldiers not only hated Galba for his choice of Piso but were also furious that he reneged on a promise of bonus pay to the troops, announcing, "It is my custom to levy [i.e., conscript] troops, not to buy them!"[4] Having alienated the military, Galba was doomed. On the morning of January 15, 69 CE, Galba and Piso entered the Forum and were attacked by soldiers who "hacked him to pieces" and decapitated Piso.[5]

The Jewish historian Josephus briefly recounts Galba's reign, as well as his death, noting that the soldiers took Galba to be *tapeinophrosynē*.[6] I've noted how the apostle Paul advocated for *tapeinophrosynē*, which New Testament translators understand as "low-thinking," or "humility" (e.g., Phil 2:3; see also 1 Pet 5:5). Josephus, however, uses *tapeinophrosynē* in the sense of "small-minded," indicating fear and inflexibility. William Whitson translates *tapeinophrosynē* in Josephus as "pusillanimous," which means "timid" or "lacking resolve," derived from Latin *pusillus*, "small," and *animus*, "mind."[7] Josephus's use of *tapeinophrosynē*, compared to that of Paul and Peter in the New Testament, reflects the generally negative connotations of the term within the Roman world. Reinhard Feldmeier, observing that both Josephus and the Stoic philosopher Epictetus employ *tapeinophrosynē*, concludes, "It has a negative meaning that lies, depending on the context, somewhere between sycophancy and pusillanimity, servility, and shabbiness."[8]

Ironically, Peter and Paul both reinterpret the word that Josephus uses to describe a pitiful leader. Godly leadership reframes

---

[3]Grant, *Twelve Caesars*, 183-84.

[4]Suetonius, *Twelve Caesars*, 258.

[5]Grant, *Twelve Caesars*, 186.

[6]Josephus, *Jewish War* 4.9.2

[7]William Whitson, trans., *The Works of Josephus: Complete and Unabridged* (Peabody, MA: Hendrickson, 1988), 688.

[8]Reinhard Feldmeier, *Power, Service, Humility: A New Testament Ethic* (Waco, TX: Baylor University Press, 2014), 61.

tapeinophrosynē, rejecting the notions of small-mindedness, weakness, and timidity while embracing self-sacrifice, gentleness, and fearless advocacy on behalf of the vulnerable. Rather than *tapeinophrosynē* describing the insecurities and other weaknesses apparent in Galba's leadership, it describes the humility necessary for guiding people on the path of shalom, or wholeness. Indeed, Christian leaders are those whose task is to shepherd, or guide, rather than cajole, harass, and humiliate.

Leadership Means Shepherding

Geometry students know that every square is a rhombus, but not every rhombus is a square. Similarly, every shepherd is a leader, but not every leader is a shepherd. Shepherds, or pastors, are leaders whether or not they have been given that official designation by a church or denomination because they possess a gift from the Holy Spirit. Spirit-empowered shepherds are drawn into relationships in which they care for others, offer guidance, and help protect people's bodies and psyches. Any of us who've been involved in a Christian community for more than a short time can name people who are pastors but did not have the title. By contrast, we are also aware of people who have titles associated with leadership or who gain positions of authority but do not have the charism of shepherd.

While the noun "shepherd" or "pastor" (*poimēn*) is used only in Ephesians 4:11 to refer to spiritual leaders other than Jesus, the verb "to shepherd" (*poimainō*) is used a few times to indicate the work of spiritual leaders (Jn 21:16; Acts 20:28; 1 Pet 5:2). Despite Ephesians 4:11 being the only place in the New Testament that speaks of a pastor as a spiritual leader, the role of pastor has been a prominent, though not always popular, part of society for centuries.[9] Paul's mention of pastors and teachers in Ephesians 4:11

[9]For a detailed discussion of the role of pastor versus the charism of shepherding, see my chapter "Guarding the Flock," in *Living the King Jesus Gospel: Discipleship and Ministry Then*

is connected to the shepherd thread that is woven throughout the Scriptures.

"The LORD is my shepherd," the opening of Psalm 23, is familiar to many, including those who might not attend church regularly. The Old Testament frequently pictures God as a shepherd, an image that describes nurture, care, and protection, not weakness. For example, Isaiah 40:11 contains a tender image of God:

> He will feed his flock like a shepherd;
> he will gather the lambs in his arms,
> and carry them in his bosom,
> and gently lead the mother sheep.

This encouraging picture of God's advent in Zion immediately follows a description of God's strength in Isaiah 40:10:

> See, the Lord GOD comes with might,
> and his arm rules for him;
> his reward is with him,
> and his recompense before him.

Ezekiel 34:11-16 is another passage emphasizing God's tender care for God's people. In the Ezekiel context, God's people had gone into exile in Babylon, but God promises to take on the role of shepherd, seeking out the sheep (Ezek 34:11-12), leading them and feeding them (Ezek 34:13-14), providing rest and physical care (Ezek 34:15-16). In the way that God is shepherd, the leaders of God's people in the Old Testament were to be shepherds for their fellow Israelites (e.g., Jer 23:4; Zech 10:2). God's anger is kindled against shepherds who forfeit, neglect, or corrupt their role (e.g., Ezek 34:10; Zech 10:3).

Jesus Christ is the model for spiritual leaders, and pastor, or shepherd, describes his character and ministry. In John 10:11, 14,

---

and Now, ed. Nijay K. Gupta, Tara Beth Leach, Matthew W. Bates, and Drew J. Strait (Eugene, OR: Cascade, 2021), 80-96.

Jesus declares himself to be the good shepherd. The apostle Peter, along with the writer of Hebrews, refer to Jesus as a shepherd (1 Pet 2:25; Heb 13:20). Peter offers a connection between shepherding and humility, following from the example of Jesus.[10] Near the end of 1 Peter, the apostle emphasizes the exemplary role that church leaders should have:

> Now as an elder myself and a witness of the sufferings of Christ, as well as one who shares in the glory to be revealed, I exhort the elders among you to tend the flock of God that is in your charge, exercising the oversight, not under compulsion but willingly, as God would have you do it—not for sordid gain but eagerly. Do not lord it over those in your charge, but be examples to the flock. And when the chief shepherd appears, you will win the crown of glory that never fades away. (1 Pet 5:1-4)

Peter addresses the entire community in 1 Peter 5, but he starts out with a focus on leadership, with humility as a theme of this exhortation. Like Jesus, leaders should not use their authority to elevate themselves or "lord it over others" but to humbly demonstrate love. Peter begins by acknowledging that he witnessed Christ's sufferings, as suffering is a theme throughout the entire letter of 1 Peter. Peter reminds his readers that their Savior shares in their reality of societal alienation, as he was abused, whipped, and executed. As an elder himself, Peter urges fellow elders to be good shepherds.

Because I grew up in New York City, and not on a farm, I have learned about sheep from other people, not from personal experience. I've often heard preachers and teachers assert that sheep are stupid animals, joking about how even dogs can lead sheep to

---

[10]Recognizing the scholarly debate surrounding the authorship of 1 Peter, I consider the Peter of the Gospels to be the author.

food and safety. However, some experts reject the assertion that sheep are unintelligent.[11] The critical issue for sheep appears to be their lack of defensive capabilities. In other words: sheep are vulnerable. The Bible's frequent references to people as sheep is not a muted insult, stigmatizing us as foolish or hard-headed. The image of sheep is meant to evoke sympathy, not ridicule or even pity, because the metaphor indicates how we can become prone to all manner of attacks. We are all sheep who need the care and guidance of good shepherds because we are susceptible to abuse—physically, emotionally, and spiritually. The good shepherd, who has experienced suffering, feels and understands the needs of vulnerable sheep. Indeed, Jesus is the Lamb of God in John's Gospel and Revelation (e.g., Jn 1:29, 36; Rev 5:6, 8, 13), whose suffering provides salvation for all who believe.

In 1 Peter 5, the apostle not only recollects Christ's sufferings but also remembers his own call to ministry after the crucifixion and resurrection of Jesus, as the command in 1 Peter 5:2 recalls John 21:1-19. The resurrected Jesus met one morning with some of his original twelve disciples after they had been fishing during the night. The disciples did not at first recognize Jesus on the lakeshore and were having no success catching any fish until after they took the apparent stranger's advice to cast their nets over the starboard side of the boat. It was then Peter realized that it was Jesus who had called to them from the shore. The disciples hauled in 153 fish, an especially good catch.

After sharing a meal with his disciples, Jesus initiated a conversation with Peter, essentially asking him the same question three times: "Do you love me?" Three times Peter responded with, "Lord, you know that I love you." With each of Peter's answers,

[11]Harriet Constable, "Sheep Are Not Stupid, and They Are Not Helpless Either," *The Independent*, April 27, 2017, https://m.theindependentbd.com/arcprint/details/91992/2017-04-27 (originally published by the BBC).

Jesus challenged him, "Feed my sheep." John 21:17 points out that "Peter was hurt because Jesus asked him the third time, 'Do you love me'?" (NIV). Peter's pain was likely due to remembering his denial of the Lord three times as Jesus was being abused and about to be crucified (Jn 13:38). The Lord did not cast Peter aside but summoned him to shepherd God's people. Peter took up that call from Jesus, and in 1 Peter 5:1-4 he passes it on to the leaders of congregations in ancient Turkey.

The term "elder" refers to someone who is older in years, and also describes a person with spiritual authority, analogous to the practice in ancient Israel (e.g., Lev 4:15; Num 11:16; Josh 8:33). The elders, being leaders, are admonished to pay attention to the areas of pride that are prone to plague people with authority. Elders must not have the wrong attitude about serving—doing it out of a sense of obligation and not out of a willing acceptance of a call from God. Some church leaders receive a salary and some volunteer their services. In either case, leaders should sense a call from God to serve people and not be domineering or coercive. And because their role is entrusted to them by God, they can't take pride in thinking that they are personally superior to those they're leading.

James 3:1 offers this caution: "Not many of you should become teachers, my brothers and sisters, for you know that we who teach will be judged with greater strictness." The apostle Paul wrote to his protégé Timothy that good character is of chief concern when selecting church leaders (1 Tim 3:1-13). Pastors and other leaders should not serve because there is no one else around, or because the church bylaws require a particular number of officers. People should not take on the role of pastor or elder simply because they are good organizers or know how to run meetings. Elders, as shepherds, are called to tend God's flock, providing oversight.

In 1 Peter 5:2 Peter uses a form of the Greek word *episkopeō* (one who watches over, or guards), from which we get the word *episcopal*, to describe the oversight leaders are to have. He uses the same root in 1 Peter 2:25, along with "shepherd" (*poimēn*), to describe Jesus: "For 'you were like sheep going astray,' but now you have returned to the Shepherd and Overseer of your souls" (NIV). Those who humbly shepherd the people of God, providing guidance, instruction, and care, lead in the same manner as Jesus.

Shepherds Foster Mutuality

The apostle Paul is not the only New Testament writer to push for mutuality among his readers. We've already seen how Pastor Paul presses for unity among the Philippians as he urges them from a faraway prison to give him joyful satisfaction by being of the same mind, possessing mutual love, and finding concord (Phil 2:2). The apostle presses on with the radical injunction to "do nothing from selfish ambition or conceit, but in humility regard others as better than yourselves" (Phil 2:3). Similarly, Paul argues for reconciliation for the Corinthian Christians, especially in 1 Corinthians.

Beyond the commands for unity that leaders make is the example they provide through the way they live. Paul typically followed his own guidance in his sacrificial ministry and partnership with others. In the previous section I noted how Peter relied on Jesus as the ultimate example of shepherding. Jesus not only taught about shepherding, but he modeled it with his life. I turn now to the book of James for an example of humble leadership that fosters mutuality.

James urges and teaches about prayer near the end of his letter. In James 5:13-18, prayer is critical for healing, with spiritual health included in the admonition of James 5:16: "Therefore confess your sins to one another, and pray for one another, so that you may be healed." Not only do sick physical bodies need to be healed, so do sick souls, which James might have in view (cf. Jas 5:19-20). Scot

McKnight highlights James's linking healing to forgiveness.[12] Confessing sins to a priest is part of regular church practice for some Christians, as McKnight notes in his comments about the sacrament of penance, or reconciliation.[13] My concern at present is not only the value of confessing sins, but the mutuality stressed in James 5:16. Confession of sin and prayer go together, and James commands that both occur with *one another*.

Given that the elders have just been mentioned in James 5:14, they are certainly included within *one another*. Elders are not leaders who tell others what to do, but they ought to engage in mutual confession and prayer along with everyone else in the Christian community. Some Christians have promoted—or tolerated—an unrealistic image of spiritual leaders. There have been shepherds who presented themselves as practically sinless because of their close relationship with God. Such is the case with groups we might label as *cults*, like the Peoples Temple and their general acceptance of Jim Jones's megalomania. The phrase "drinking the Kool-Aid" is part of our lexicon in the United States and emerges from the outrageous episode in Jonestown, Guyana, when over nine hundred people drank a poison concoction—most of them apparently voluntarily—under Jim Jones's instructions. The horrible incident happened during my senior year of high school and remains for me a constant point of fascination and caution.[14] Yet even some churches that have resisted the extremes of the Peoples Temple can grant their leaders so much leeway that their sins get overlooked and their commands are unquestioned. Humility requires that *one another* applies to shepherds as well as sheep.

---

[12]Scot McKnight, *The Letter of James*, New International Commentary on the New Testament (Grand Rapids, MI: Eerdmans, 2011), 447.

[13]McKnight, *James*, 446.

[14]Jeff Guinn, *The Road to Jonestown: Jim Jones and Peoples Temple* (New York: Simon & Schuster, 2017), is an engaging, detailed account of the life of Jim Jones and what led to the infamous mass suicide in Jonestown.

Often church attendees seek out spiritual leaders to pray for and with them, but they might never hear those leaders acknowledge their own sins. I have heard public apologies of some celebrity pastors in the wake of scandal, but rarely have I heard confessions within the congregations that I attended. In recent years we might get the nonapology that is framed as confession, such as, "I'm sorry if anyone was hurt by what I did," rather than the leader owning their transgression.

During my years of pastoral ministry, I was reluctant to admit mistakes or specific sins for fear of being publicly shamed or having people lose confidence in me as a leader. It was not until I was older, closer to my last decade of full-time pastoral ministry, that I discovered the power of confessing sins to people, in addition to God. My confessions did not typically occur in a Sunday worship gathering, but with some configuration of my staff team or volunteer leaders. It is not easy, and causes me varying degrees of angst, but I know that confession builds trust. Mutual confession and prayer are some of humility's fruit.

There is a scene in an episode of the television show *Ted Lasso* when Ted and his fellow coaches are about to follow the players out of the locker room for a match, but everyone knows that Ted is struggling with something, so there is an aura of discomfort surrounding them all. Ted musters the courage to share his personal struggle and that he had been lying about it. Suddenly, each man in the room unloads some emotional burden—in the form of a confession. When the head coach opened up, the others found it easier to be vulnerable.

Humble leaders are honest, and that invites honesty from others. Humble leaders understand how risky it can be to confess their sins and to pray honestly, so those leaders can help to provide nonthreatening environments that allow for mutual confession. In healthy families, when parents make mistakes or exasperate their children, they apologize, even though such a thing was rare in my childhood. In such situations, children do not lose respect for their parents but are pulled even closer and are more likely to confess their own failings. Healthy Christian communities similarly foster strong bonds when those who shepherd the flock set the example of mutual confession and prayer.

Shepherds Serve

In the Greco-Roman world of Jesus and his followers, *tapeinophrosynē*, as I noted with the example of Emperor Galba, was not used to describe virtuous behavior. In that world, much as in ours, people vigorously pursue honor. One could achieve honor through ostensibly selfless acts, such as heroic deeds in warfare or paying money to meet a public need. In contrast, putting others first or voluntarily taking a lowly position was dishonorable. Jesus, however, taught otherwise. In Luke 22:24-27, Jesus makes a distinction between the Roman style of leadership and his practice, which his followers were to emulate:

> A dispute also arose among them as to which one of them was to be regarded as the greatest. But he said to them, "The kings of the Gentiles lord it over them; and those in authority over them are called benefactors. But not so with you; rather the greatest among you must become like the youngest, and the leader like one who serves. For who is greater, the one who is at the table or the one who serves? Is it not the one at the table? But I am among you as one who serves.

Jesus' teaching about service is a response to an argument among the disciples regarding status. Luke uses the rare word *philoneikia* (love of strife), which occurs in the New Testament only here, to describe the tension.[15] The disciples are being

[15]Joseph A. Fitzmyer, *The Gospel According to Luke: Introduction, Translation, and Notes*, Anchor Bible 28A (Garden City, NY: Doubleday, 1981), 1416. The adjective *philoneikos* occurs in 1 Cor

vainglorious. They are consumed with how others view them, being concerned about *the appearance* of greatness. We have had politicians in the modern era argue over the size of the crowds they addressed as an indicator of their greatness. Perhaps closer to home are Christian leaders in churches and other organizations who desire the appearance of greatness, so they strive to be seen near public officials or to have their names or works prominently displayed. Our competitive society does not always expect greatness but will settle for *the appearance* of greatness in the absence of the real thing.

According to Jesus, Gentile kings, or literally "kings of the nations," are authoritarian and lord it over others. These leaders give themselves honorific titles, calling themselves benefactors. The noun "benefactor" (*euergetēs*) occurs only here in the New Testament but was a title given to gods, princes, and emperors in the Greco-Roman world.[16] The way of the world is to appear great, take on your own title, and dominate others. Galba is but one example among many of those who exploited their power and position for prominence or personal gain. Caesar Augustus, the Roman emperor when Jesus was born, according to Luke 2:1, despite being given the name Octavian was called Augustus (Latin for "venerable") and referred to as a benefactor. But the disciples of Jesus must not behave the same way; they are to be like the youngest and the servant—those ranked low in social standing.

Some might read these verses as a strategy for achieving greatness: act low and you'll go high in the world. However, Jesus does not seem to care about becoming great in the way society measures greatness. Jesus redefines greatness by using himself as

11:16. See also John T. Carroll, *Luke: A Commentary*, New Testament Library (Louisville, KY: Westminster John Knox, 2012), 438, who describes the situation as "verbal sparring" on the part of the disciples.

[16]Fitzmyer, *Luke*, 1417.

a counterexample. According to the world's reckoning, the one who reclines at the table is greater than the one serving the table. Yet Jesus came to serve (see Mk 10:45). Jesus' service, however, was not part of a strategy to gain an advantageous position. The Son of God demonstrated that greatness is measured in service to others and any honor, or "greatness" that comes is because God gives grace to the humble (cf. Prov 3:34). God's grace, however, is not necessarily worldly prominence; it takes a variety of forms. As with Jesus, greatness might mean contributing to a more just society without ever holding a political office, earning large sums of money, or achieving notoriety. God's eternal rewards are imperishable.

There seem to be few models of noncoercive leadership in our society, but Jesus is such a model because he demonstrates that shepherding is nonabusive, humble, and great. We need shepherds who understand what it means to serve, and many of the best shepherds come from the lowest segments of society because people who serve understand what it takes to help others become their best selves. Jesus is Lord and all power is his; however, he does not guide through domination and intimidation, but through love. Humble shepherds lead in the manner of Jesus and not in the common, often authoritarian way of our society.

Shepherds Are Authentic

When people around us think that strong leadership requires a dictatorial approach rather than a collaborative one, we might question if the Jesus way of leadership is effective. Of course, that depends on how we define *effective*. If our goal is to help each other become more like Jesus and demonstrate God's love for the world through caring, healing, and liberating, then we can be comfortable with a nondictatorial style of leadership.

In my own journey as a pastor, I sought to be collaborative, but some church leaders, often enamored of the worlds of business or the military, viewed my style as weak. In time, I became more comfortable with what appeared weak because my style helped to engage people in fellowship and service. In my last pastorate, before becoming a full-time seminary professor, I met with the church's leadership team to discuss the pastoral transition. One member of that team, a young woman the age of my oldest child, made a passing comment that I lead "with open hands." I hold that comment dear and will never forget it because she expressed as a value something that had been viewed by some as a shortcoming, but which I knew reflected the Jesus way of shepherding. For this young woman, leading with open hands meant collaboration, serving, and authenticity.

In what some have considered Paul's first letter, 1 Thessalonians, the apostle encourages the converts who have turned from idolatry (1 Thess 1:9) despite persecution (1 Thess 1:6), and attempts to clarify their understanding, especially regarding eschatological matters (1 Thess 4:13). Paul also describes his ministry, along with that of coworkers Silas and Timothy (1 Thess 1:1). Beverly Gaventa asserts that Paul contrasts the ministry "with the charges sometimes made against wandering philosophers. Paul and his associates are not abusive, greedy, seeking for glory. Instead, they are apostles of Christ."[17] In 1 Thessalonians 2:5-8 Paul emphasizes the authentic, relational nature of apostolic ministry:

> As you know and as God is our witness, we never came with words of flattery or with a pretext for greed; nor did we seek praise from mortals, whether from you or from others, though we might have made demands as apostles of Christ. But we were gentle among you, like a nurse tenderly caring for her own children. So deeply do we care for you that we

[17]Beverly Roberts Gaventa, *Our Mother Saint Paul* (Louisville: Westminster John Knox, 2007), 26.

> are determined to share with you not only the gospel of God but also our own selves, because you have become very dear to us.

Astute Bible readers will note that the NRSV text that I cited comes with a footnote: the word "gentle" (*ēpioi*) in 1 Thessalonians 2:7 could read "infants" (*nēpioi*). It is difficult to know what Paul's original word was because both readings are well-attested in ancient manuscripts. Nijay K. Gupta provides a thorough examination of the issues surrounding the textual variant.[18] While many scholars conclude that Paul wrote *nēpioi*, resolving the issue isn't necessary for our purposes, as either word "gentle" or "infants" reinforces the authenticity described in the entire paragraph. Both metaphors, as Gupta relays, "are similar in terms of intimacy and tenderness."[19]

Apostolic intimacy and tenderness are especially evident in 1 Thessalonians 2:8, where discipleship is shown to consist of sharing life, not just words. Humble people give of their time, allowing others a window into their lives. Not every person will—or should—have unfettered access to all the intimate details of our lives because not everyone is mature enough to be trusted with our feelings, our family's concerns, or other sensitive matters. Of course, I do not refer to abusive or other illegal or immoral behaviors that ought to be brought to light and speedily addressed. But immature, irresponsible, or antagonistic people might gossip, make assumptions, exaggerate an issue, or even slander us. If I share that I've argued with my wife, for example, someone lacking maturity might have some people thinking we're heading to divorce court! We learn to develop healthy boundaries. Yet the best way for Christians to grow as disciples is through relationships,

---

[18]Nijay K. Gupta, *1 & 2 Thessalonians*, Zondervan Critical Introductions to the New Testament (Grand Rapids, MI: Zondervan, 2019), 106-14.

[19]Gupta, *1 & 2 Thessalonians*, 114.

and those who have been traveling the journey for a greater amount of time—elders—shepherd others by being with them and not just talking at them.

Shepherding in Practice

Affirming words, an overwhelming number of educational resources, and countless role models conspire to teach those in the majority culture in the United States, especially men in that group, that the world belongs to them.[20] White people were taught a myth of meritocracy—that if they worked hard, they could get or become whatever they wanted.

A scandal was uncovered in 2018, revealing how some wealthy White people—including well-recognized television personalities—had cheated to get their children into college. Some of the activity included students receiving scholarships for sports they did not play, parents paying for impostors to pose as their children in order to take entrance exams, and college officials receiving bribes. In one case, an actress paid $15,000 for a proctor to change her daughter's SAT answers.[21]

One thing that the scandal revealed is the myth of meritocracy. The United States was created for the success of White people, particularly men. The data shows that White men are substantially less likely to be jailed than African American men or Latinos.[22] Whites are not typically racially profiled by authorities. There are a host of advantages that White people have in our society. I can't recount the

[20]For some elaboration and illustration of this assertion, see Jonathan Walton, *Twelve Lies That Hold America Captive: And the Truth That Sets Us Free* (Downers Grove, IL: InterVarsity Press, 2018), 62-76.

[21]Bill Chappell and Merrit Kennedy, "U.S. Charges Dozens of Parents, Coaches in Massive College Admissions Scandal," *NPR*, March 12, 2019, www.npr.org/2019/03/12/702539140/u-s-accuses-actresses-others-of-fraud-in-wide-college-admissions-scandal.

[22]Pew Research Center, "Blacks and Hispanics Are Overrepresented in U.S. Prisons," January 12, 2018, www.pewresearch.org/short-reads/2019/04/30/shrinking-gap-between-number-of-blacks-and-whites-in-prison/; NAACP, "Criminal Justice Fact Sheet," accessed February 15, 2023, www.naacp.org/criminal-justice-fact-sheet/.

number of times White men have assumed that I should move out of their way on a sidewalk, have mistaken me for "the help," or have beckoned me across the room with their hands—all gestures that are a byproduct of their position in society, but which I imagine they don't think twice about. Perhaps humility is a concept that White people, especially men, need to cultivate in light of society's inequity.

Christians give lip service to the notion of leaders being servants but have an ambiguous view of the role of humility, often seeing humility as how we manage worldly success rather than how we give of ourselves to God and others.[23] During my years of pastoral ministry it was easy to develop a leadership inferiority complex. My peers were frequently touting some book, conference, or workshop designed to make me a better leader. For many years of my pastoral ministry, I could not afford to buy media resources or attend most of the conferences, but I also could not help having a fear of missing out. I feared missing out on some silver bullet that would make my church grow larger. After all, the bottom line of the church leadership industrial complex is bigger churches. Church leadership conferences pushed the messaging typical of what we generally receive in the United States: bigger is better.

I learned, however, that bigger churches are not necessarily better churches. Sometimes bigger can mean disproportionate and unhealthy, like a cancerous tumor. Large institutions can mask the true character of their leaders. There are, however, times when we can see plainly the duplicitous character of a leader, yet they still amass a large following. The teachings of Jesus and the apostles do not disparage large numbers of worshipers; however,

---

[23]See Jane Foulcher, *Reclaiming Humility: Four Studies in the Monastic Tradition*, Cistercian Studies 255 (Collegeville, MN: Cistercian Publications, 2015), 3: "While it is common to recognize a certain sense of personal modesty in the people we most admire, we tend to be suspicious of anything that diminishes self-actualization. Ironically, in Western culture the word *humility* is used most comfortably as a way of portraying an individual's gracious bearing of success."

the New Testament does prioritize discipleship over attendance and utilizes shepherding as a chief image for the work of discipleship that leaders are to perform.

Shepherding describes the essence of discipleship, which is the care and guidance of God's people. Leaders might acquire notoriety through attracting large numbers of church attendees, but while such notoriety can elevate one's social status, it can also foster attitudes and practices that oppose humility. There are far too many examples of Christian leaders who, contrary to the teachings of the New Testament and example of Jesus, abuse the power associated with their positions. More shameful than abusive and narcissistic leaders are the sycophants who allow such leaders to flourish. Organizations including churches, nonprofit ministries, and even governments demonstrate that regardless of written values or internal structures designed for "checks and balances," unhealthy leaders are immune to censure as long as there are plenty of donors.

Effective Christian leadership, however, does not focus on numbers, but rather on people learning who they are and what they're capable of doing. Christian shepherds should be part of a team because leadership is collaborative and as such requires humility.[24] Collaborative leadership requires humble pastors who not only understand but also accept that shepherding means following the model of Jesus.

One leader I consider to be effective is a friend who represents a host of ministers who serve faithfully in relative obscurity. Pastor Randy Heacock, currently at the Doylestown Mennonite Church in Pennsylvania, is a humble, emotionally healthy leader who

[24]See Graham N. Standish, *Humble Leadership: Being Radically Open to God's Guidance and Grace* (Herndon, VA: Alban Institute, 2007), and Joseph H. Hellerman, *Embracing Shared Ministry: Power and Status in the Early Church and Why It Matters Today* (Grand Rapids, MI: Kregel, 2013).

listens well, leads with integrity, speaks truthfully, and is respected by most who know him. I've had the privilege of knowing Randy for over twenty-five years when he was serving in northern Virginia and I in Washington, DC, and have witnessed the way he collaborates with a variety of people, builds quality relationships with people outside of his congregation, respects other humans, and genuinely represents Jesus without being fixated on accumulating wealth, power, or status. Randy is a pastor worth emulating because of his humility, not primarily because of his preaching, business acumen, or his strategies for increasing church attendance. I realize that it's Randy's humility that has made it easy for me to accept his counsel. He is a good and faithful servant whose words and actions point people to Jesus.

Chapter Six

Enduring

Putting Our Suffering into Perspective

For humility alone escapes all the snares of the Devil and vanquishes his power.

Thomas à Kempis

At one time or another we have all felt overwhelmed by life's trials, or we tried to accompany someone in that predicament. It took every ounce of strength to persevere, every grain of mustard-seed-sized faith, every molecule of hope, and every atom of courage to endure. I am reluctant to recount specific experiences of suffering for fear of triggering some degree of posttraumatic stress disorder. But I am sure your mind has already traveled to some painful memory because that is the way trauma works. I regret that you have experienced pain, and I commend you for your perseverance.

Suffering is serious and not frivolous. Suffering is not being stuck in traffic or dealing with other mundane inconveniences. Suffering is life-threatening and frightening. Humans remain Satan's perpetual targets, and we stand up to demonic assaults, until

Thomas à Kempis, *Recommendatio humilitatis* 72, 75 (trans. Brian McNeil), cited in Reinhard Feldmeier, *Power, Service, Humility: A New Testament Ethic* (Waco, TX: Baylor University Press, 2014), 93.

the day of the Lord when God will wipe away every tear from our eyes (see Rev 7:17; 21:4). Although followers of Jesus have been liberated from sin's dominion, we presently live with the reality of evil, which jeopardizes the joy our union with Christ is meant to give us. We regularly pray, "Deliver us from evil" because evil (and the evil one) is relentless. The problem of evil is that it exists simultaneously with an all-loving, all-knowing, and all-powerful God. Evil confronts us daily even while philosophers and theologians try to unravel the problem of evil. As Eliphaz the Temanite asserts in the book of Job, "Human beings are born to trouble just as sparks fly upward" (Job 5:7).

As a result of years of pastoral ministry, I'm convinced that our main reaction to suffering should not be to ignore it, rationalize it, or even attempt to learn from it. Those reactions are often blithely encouraged by well-intentioned onlookers who do not know what to say in the face of suffering. Our friends can be like Job's, attempting to offer some rationale for our suffering, including pointing fingers of incrimination at us. Proponents of the so-called prosperity gospel essentially deny the reality of suffering, much like the founders of Christian Science, who denied the reality of evil.[1] Our friends who have been influenced by prosperity teaching might blame us for our own predicament, accusing us of insufficient faith or of holding on to some sin. We might come to believe, "Surely I must have caused these problems!" Or we begin to wonder if our faith in Jesus has been futile. Other onlookers hasten to point out the lessons we are supposed to learn, even to the point of asserting that suffering is good.

---

[1]"If God, or good, is real, then evil, the unlikeness of God, is unreal. And evil can only seem to be real by giving reality to the unreal." Mary Baker Eddy, *Science and Health with Key to the Scriptures* (Boston: Christian Science Publishing Company, 1875), www.christianscience.com/the-christian-science-pastor/science-and-health/chapter-xiv-recapitulation?citation=SH%20470:11-470:20.

Suffering is not good. We know that fire can be dangerous without having to put our hands into the flames. Our main reaction to suffering is to fight for survival. We need to manage as best we can, feeling our way through the darkness until the light appears. Endurance is our goal. Endurance is required in all difficulties as we strive to break free and even as we somehow find resolution. Our task is to hold on, to cling tenaciously to God, and do our best not to give up. We do not rush to identify whatever lessons there might be to learn. Judith Lewis Herman, in *Trauma and Recovery*, delineates that "recovery unfolds in three stages. The central task of the first stage is the establishment of safety."[2] It is possible that good may come from evil, but the first order of business is survival. We endure as we find safety, and we continue to endure until we establish a new normal that might be called ordinary life.

I hasten to add that I am in no way advocating that people should remain in abusive or dangerous situations. I condemn any counsel that God wants people to remain with abusive spouses or in other oppressive situations. We must break free from abuse as soon as we are able, and that move toward wholeness requires courage. Humility can empower us to exercise courage, a topic I address in chapter nine.

Joseph, the son of patriarch Jacob, had ten jealous older brothers who sold him into slavery (Gen 37:5-36). Eventually, after tumultuous years that included being the victim of sexual harassment, false accusations, imprisonment, and delayed promises, Joseph could testify to his brothers, "Even though you intended to do harm to me, God intended it for good" (Gen 50:20). We must not, however, rush to the end of Joseph's story and minimize his years of struggle.

[2]Judith Lewis Herman, *Trauma and Recovery* (New York: Basic Books, 2015), 155. Herman proceeds to explain that "the central task of the second stage is remembrance and mourning. The central task of the third stage is reconnection with ordinary life."

That tendency to rush to the end is reflected in the way that many people recount the story of Job. They emphasize that at the beginning of the story God permitted Satan to attack Job (Job 1:1–2:13) but at the end made up for Job's losses by blessing him with new children and twice the possessions he had at the start (Job 42:10-17). That happily ever after fairy-tale retelling of Job not only minimizes the nearly forty chapters between the beginning and the end but also fails to empathize with Job's trauma of losing children and possessions even though he was "blameless and upright, one who feared God and turned away from evil" (Job 1:1).

We all want a happy ending—sooner rather than later—so we hasten to quote Romans 8:28 that "we know that all things work together for good for those who love God, who are called according to his purpose." It is wonderful indeed to know that we might realize eventual blessings and be able to look back on suffering with thanksgiving. But such gratitude comes with hindsight, while trouble is the present view for the sufferer. While in the thick of suffering we don't rush to lessons to be learned. We practice endurance, a skill that comes from having cultivated humility.

Humility enables us to find—and perhaps even feel—the presence of God in the midst of our struggles. Humility invites us to focus on the most important elements of life and helps us find kindred spirits who bolster our faith, who listen more than speak, who pray without being cajoled, and who remind us that we are never alone even though we "walk through the valley of the shadow of death" (Ps 23:4 KJV). Humility brings God's grace, even in the pain.

Several New Testament writings place endurance through suffering at the forefront. For example, the letters of James and 1 Peter aim to encourage Christians to remain steadfast in their faith even as they experience trials. Humility is not likely to be the first thought that comes to mind when we are suffering, but James and 1 Peter can help us to discover humility's role in the perseverance necessary to endure suffering.

Endurance in James

Immediately at the outset of his letter, James offers both encouragement and challenging advice to "the twelve tribes in the Dispersion" (Jas 1:1-27). Trials are inevitable; humans "fall into" (*peripiptō*) them (Jas 1:2). The verb *peripiptō* is rare in the New Testament, appearing only twice outside James 1:2. In Luke 10:30, the beginning of the parable of the good Samaritan, *peripiptō* refers to a physical assault. It is not the victim's fault that he "fell among" thieves. In Acts 27:41, the verb refers to a boating accident resulting from a storm. *Peripiptō* describes the randomness of trials.

James encourages joy not because trials are fun or inherently good but because they provide an opportunity for our faith to push us toward maturity. Despite the inexorable nature of trials, we persevere through them. Perseverance, or patient endurance, is not passivity, but is active submission to God. As we humbly yield to God, whether we fight or take flight, we find divine power to negotiate our situation. For James, humility propels us to focus on God and God's word. This focus invites us to reaffirm our allegiance to the Lord, and with that reaffirmation we refine our perspectives on life's important matters. At some future point, when our strength has been renewed, we will be able to look back to see what God did in and through us. Trials can make us mature (Jas 1:4), wise (Jas 1:5), and resistant to doubleminded doubting (Jas 1:6-7).

In James 1:9 the economically impoverished "lowly" (*tapeinos*) stand in contrast to the materially "rich." James urges the impoverished believers to boast in their elevated spiritual position, which stands in contrast to the morally deficient position of the exploitative rich (Jas 2:5-7; 5:1-6). Lowliness in James 1:9 is not a voluntary posture, but the result of injustice.[3] The lowly—the economically disadvantaged—are vulnerable, but God is on their side. James echoes Jesus in the Sermon on the Mount: "Blessed are the poor in spirit, for theirs is the kingdom of heaven" (Mt 5:3); and "Blessed are the meek, for they will inherit the earth" (Mt 5:5). Those suffering because of financial insecurity can ironically boast—not in their own abilities, but in God's care.

James gives this admonition because God's care isn't always evident during suffering. Humble circumstances can foster humility because God raises up the lowly. Humility allows us to witness the hand of God even when suffering unjustly, and also urges us to find sustenance from Scripture. In James 1:21, the "implanted word" refers to Scripture's teachings embraced by followers of Jesus.[4] We welcome God's word with meekness (*prautēs*) in order to combat the resentments that can propagate from trials and temptations (Jas 1:12-21). Deliverance, according to James 1:21, comes through the power of God's word and humility allows us to experience that salvation.

Humility and deliverance are also linked in James 4:6-8 (NRSVUE), where yielding to God is connected to resisting the devil:

> But God gives all the more grace; therefore it says,
>
> "God opposes the proud
> but gives grace to the humble."
>
> Submit yourselves therefore to God. Resist the devil, and he will flee from you. Draw near to God, and he will draw near to you. Cleanse your hands, you sinners, and purify your hearts, you double-minded.

---

[3]James 1:9 is an example of how *tapeinos* can describe humiliation as well as voluntary submission.

[4]Luke Timothy Johnson, *The Letter of James: A New Translation with Introduction and Commentary*, Anchor Bible 37A (New York: Doubleday, 1995), 202.

The devil flees when we resist. Our adrenaline-fueled response to hardships—even those coming through the devil's direct assault—might be to fight or to flee. Fighting is often toe to toe, slinging the same weapons used against us. When we are slandered, we respond with vitriol; when we are assaulted, we might reach for a weapon. But we ought not try to fight with carnal weapons (2 Cor 10:4). Flight should take us away from abuse and toward God, but not cause us to abandon our commitment to Christ or to God's word. As in the parable of the seeds, sometimes the trials of life cause the rootless person to fall away (Mt 13:20-21). Sadly, there have been many who gave up on Jesus altogether because of life's difficulties. For James, humility includes drawing near to God (Jas 4:8). Yielding or submitting to God and nearness to God are part of what it means to resist the devil. Humility can help bring deliverance from satanic harassment.

Endurance in 1 Peter

There's little question that the first readers of 1 Peter were suffering (e.g., 1 Pet 1:6; 4:12-13; 5:9). Even though we are not given all the details concerning the perpetrators of the harassment, we can read that the Christians were slandered and maligned, even if not all were physically assaulted (e.g., 1 Pet 2:12, 15, 19; 3:9, 16; 4:4). Beleaguered and vulnerable, these believers are in the unique—albeit unenviable—position of representing Jesus in hostile circumstances.

Humility is part of the strategy for endurance, according to Peter. Humility fosters community solidarity (1 Pet 3:8; see chapter three), advances the gospel of Jesus Christ (1 Pet 3:1-6, 15-16), and promotes dependence on the Lord (1 Pet 5:6). Cynicism asserts that misery loves company, but community solidarity is crucial for surviving hardships. First Peter 3:8 lists a string of solidarity-enhancing attitudes: "Finally, all of you, have unity of spirit, sympathy, love for one another, a tender heart, and a humble mind." The phrase "unity of spirit" is reminiscent of Paul's "same mind" and "one mind" language in Philippians 2:2, yet Peter uses a noun that occurs only here in the entire New Testament, *sympathēs*. The connection to the English *sympathy* is evident (see also the verb *sympatheō* in Heb 4:15; 10:34). United spirits, sibling love, and tenderheartedness must accompany "a humble mind" (*tapeinophrones*). This is another word that occurs only once in the New Testament, but it's related to Paul's *tapeinophrosynē*. Mutuality is evident in Peter's language, where humility moves beyond yielding to God to include community-enhancing actions. We might attempt to push through life's difficult times with a business-as-usual mindset, but we need others to care for us when we are hurting. Community solidarity means not only giving care to others but also humbly receiving it.

According to 1 Peter 3, those who endure suffering become living testimonies of what faith in Jesus can mean. In 1 Peter 3:1-6, Christian women married to unbelieving men are given a strategy for survival that includes humility. These Jesus-following wives were vulnerable due to the way Greco-Roman households positioned women, enslaved people, and children under the paterfamilias's authority.[5] These faithful wives, however, are evangelists and reveal that people may be "won over without a word" (1 Pet 3:1). In some contemporary Christian circles, evangelism is typically a wordy enterprise, heavily dependent on rational arguments presented in eye-catching formats. I was taught during my college years, and even early in my seminary experience, to minimize the role of an evangelist's Christlike behavior in favor of words. For

[5]There's much that can be said about the vulnerable position of these wives and the way this passage has been used to reinforce patriarchy. That is beyond this study, but see my treatment in *1 Peter*, Story of God Bible Commentary (Grand Rapids, MI: Zondervan, 2017), 127-38. Note also that Peter's words to enslaved believers, 1 Pet 2:18-25, which are likely offensive for many contemporary readers, also communicate a strategy for survival for a vulnerable population.

some, so-called friendship evangelism was presented as a strategy, but still required us to view people in our lives as targets. The wives in 1 Peter do not take on a project per se, but cultivate humility as a way of life that contributes to engendering faith in their husbands. Through their "gentle and quiet spirit," these wives demonstrate the way of Jesus (1 Pet 3:4).

"Gentle" unfortunately can evoke the notion of docility, particularly when viewed through the lens of patriarchy, but the word is used of Jesus Christ. The Lord describes himself in Matthew 11:29 as "gentle" or "meek" (*praus*), a term explored in chapter one and that can suggest dependence on God and a desire to make peace with others. "Quiet" (*ēsychios*) may be better translated as "tranquil."[6] One of the few occurrences of *ēsychios* in the Septuagint is in Isaiah 66:2: "But this is the one to whom I will look, to the humble and contrite in spirit, who trembles at my word."[7] While it is true that the women of 1 Peter 3:1-6 do not need to rely on words to convince their husbands, God is not requiring all women to keep their mouths shut whenever someone tells them to. Rather, Peter stresses the calmness of spirit characteristic of humble people because they depend on God. Indeed, gentleness and tranquility are qualities that must be internally present, in "the inner self," and are "precious in God's sight" (1 Pet 3:4).

Humility means gentleness and tranquility, begins with yielding to God, and facilitates wordless witness. Words, however, can

---

[6]See John H. Elliott, *1 Peter: A New Translation with Introduction and Commentary*, Anchor Bible 37B (New York: Doubleday, 2000), 566.

[7]In several places within the writings of the Apostolic Fathers, *praus* and *ēsychios* are paired (e.g., 1 Clement 13:4; Epistle of Barnabas 19:4). The *Shepherd of Hermas* places *praus* together with *ēsychios* as well as *tapeinophrōn* in describing the devoted disciple of Jesus: "In the first place the one who has the divine spirit from above is gentle and quiet and humble, and stays away from all evil and futile desires of this age, and considers himself to be poorer than others, and gives no answer to anyone when consulted. Nor does he speak on his own (nor does the holy spirit speak when a person wants to speak), but when God wants him to speak" (43.8, trans. Michael W. Holmes, *The Apostolic Fathers: Greek Texts and English Translations*, 2nd ed. [Grand Rapids, MI: Baker Books, 1999]). Humility in *Shepherd* appears similarly to that in 1 Peter. In both writings, humility starts as devotion to God but affects interactions with others.

become necessary, especially if Christians are called on to offer a defense of their faith (1 Pet 3:15). When naysayers malign Christians for their devotion to Jesus, we ideally respond with Christlike humility. We defend the faith with gentleness (*praus*) and reverence (1 Pet 3:16), as is true of the faithful wives' witness earlier in the chapter (1 Pet 3:3-4). For Peter's readers, gentleness characterizes devotion to God, the object of fear, or reverence (e.g., 1 Pet 2:17).[8] When confronted by those who may be hostile to our faith in Jesus, we are to respond humbly, which begins by yielding to God.

James indicated that hardships can be random, since we "fall into" them (Jas 1:2), but they can also come from the devil (Jas 4:6). Peter too mentions that the evil one is directly responsibility for some troubles because the devil, our adversary, prowls like a lion (1 Pet 5:8). Peter calls for humility among leaders as well as the entire community (1 Pet 5:5) and in 1 Peter 5:6-7 highlights dependence on the Lord. Anxiety naturally accompanies hardships, but when under pressure we might fail to acknowledge, process, or otherwise deal with our anxiety. Peter invites us to throw our cares onto the Lord, reminding us that the Lord cares for us.

It takes humility to let go of our worries. "I can do it myself" may be the mantra born of cultural expectations and not faith in God. America's rugged individualism works against humility. In our efforts to encourage independence in children, we must take care not to implant in them the false notion of self-sufficiency. Humility allows us to accept help and frees us to take our burdens to the Lord and leave them there.

The Reward of Humility

Perseverance—faithful endurance—is the goal when dealing with hardships. We ride the wave of trials rather than struggle

---

[8]See Elliott, *1 Peter*, 629.

fruitlessly against them. Yet we are never fatalistic about trials; we believe that they will end. Weeping will give way to joy and mourning to dancing (Ps 30:5, 11). Faith gives us strength to endure. Hope motivates us to hold on. Humility offers a strategy for perseverance.

Humility also brings with it the promise of God's favor. As noted in the earlier discussion of humility and the fear of the Lord (chapter one), those who submit to God experience divine favor. The straightforward declaration of Proverbs 3:34 illustrates God's delight over humility:

> Toward the scorners he is scornful,
> but to the humble he shows favor.

So paradigmatic is this axiom that its message gets repeated in several places in both canonical and noncanonical Jewish and Christian writings. In the Apocrypha, Sirach, for example, picks up this perspective on humility:

> My child, perform your tasks with humility;
> then you will be loved by those whom God accepts.
> The greater you are, the more you must humble yourself;
> so you will find favor in the sight of the Lord. (Sir 3:17-18)

Ben Sira recognizes that the difficulty associated with being humble is directly proportional to one's social status. The high and mighty disdain humility but must cultivate it. Low status in society can be related to lowliness before God.[9] For Ben Sira, God so values humility that the reward includes not only favor in God's eyes but also love from other people (Sir 3:17).[10]

[9]See Klaus Wengst, *Humility: Solidarity of the Humiliated; The Transformation of an Attitude and Its Social Relevance in Graeco-Roman, Old Testament-Jewish, and Early Christian Tradition*, trans. John Bowden (Philadelphia: Fortress, 1988). Cf. Mt 5:3; Lk 6:20.

[10]Patrick W. Skehan and Alexander A. Di Lella, *The Wisdom of Ben Sira: A New Translation with Notes*, Anchor Bible 39 (New York: Doubleday, 1987), 160.

Humility's trajectory in both the Old and New Testament includes this concept of God's reward. Note that the refrain referenced above: "God opposes the proud, but gives grace to the humble" (found in Jas 4:6 and 1 Pet 5:5) comes from Proverbs 3:34. God is against the arrogant, who are antagonistic toward God (e.g., Lk 1:51; Rom 1:30; cf. Mk 7:22). In both James 4:6 and 1 Peter 5:5, the picture of humility is framed by an attitude toward God, but as with Micah 6:8 there are implications for how others are to be treated. As we have seen, the verses immediately following James 4:6 flesh out how humility is fundamentally submission to God:

> But he gives all the more grace; therefore it says, "God opposes the proud, but gives grace to the humble." Submit yourselves therefore to God. Resist the devil, and he will flee from you. Draw near to God, and he will draw near to you. Cleanse your hands, you sinners, and purify your hearts, you double-minded. Lament and mourn and weep. Let your laughter be turned into mourning and your joy into dejection. Humble yourselves before the Lord, and he will exalt you. (Jas 4:6-10)

Reinhard Feldmeier describes how James connects humility and divine favor: "Humility is thus the condition for receiving 'grace all the more richly.' This is stated first as an obligation, and then as a promise."[11] People are obliged to yield to God, which includes resisting the devil's charms, and the promise is God's favor. Feldmeier concludes that the "central idea here is a radical self-diminution as submission to God."[12] Submission means drawing near to God, which includes acts of contrition (i.e., cleansing hands, purifying hearts, lamentation, and weeping). Repentance is an act of humility.[13]

---

[11]Feldmeier, *Power, Service, Humility*, 90.

[12]Feldmeier, *Power, Service, Humility*, 92.

[13]See Eve-Marie Becker, *Paul on Humility*, trans. Wayne Coppins, Baylor–Mohr Siebeck Studies in Early Christianity (Waco, TX: Baylor University Press, 2020), 132-33.

First Peter provides encouragement as well as instruction for weary believers who are being marginalized by the broader Roman society. Near the end of the letter, after admonishing leaders ("elders") to be good shepherds who watch over the sheep (1 Pet 5:1-4), Peter urges younger members of the community to heed their shepherds (1 Pet 5:5a). The entire community is then commanded to practice humility (1 Pet 5:5b). What becomes clear is that humility serves a unifying role as part of Peter's final words to these Christians in Asia Minor. Yet, in citing Proverbs 3:34, Peter emphasizes the correct bearing people are to have in their relationship with God. John H. Elliott notes the contrast between the arrogant and the humble and points out that "humility is the only proper stance before God and the necessary prelude and precondition to exaltation."[14]

Suffering is often the result of injustice, as those with power in a competitive society exploit those without the same amount of material resources. Part of humility's reward is knowing that unjust people will not always flourish in their wickedness. The first part of the proverb, "God opposes the proud," surely serves as a warning for those with power and social status, but it also provides a measure of comfort for those who have been victimized. God's opposition to the arrogant reminds us that God is just and will not allow evil to go unchecked. We may not always see the arrogant fall in our lifetimes, but their fall is sure to happen. Herod Agrippa's final moments, recounted in Acts 12:20-23, provide a poignant example:

> Now Herod was angry with the people of Tyre and Sidon. So they came to him in a body; and after winning over Blastus, the king's chamberlain, they asked for a reconciliation, because their country depended on the king's country for food.

---

[14]Elliott, *1 Peter*, 848.

> On an appointed day Herod put on his royal robes, took his seat on the platform, and delivered a public address to them. The people kept shouting, "The voice of a god, and not of a mortal!" And immediately, because he had not given the glory to God, an angel of the Lord struck him down, and he was eaten by worms and died. (Acts 12:20-23)

God judged Herod Agrippa's arrogance, and punishment came swiftly. There are many biblical stories of proud people facing God's opposition (e.g., 1 Sam 15:26-29; Is 14:13-15; Ezek 28:2-10). These sobering accounts illustrate Proverbs 3:34 and its echoes. Pride brings divine resistance, which results in disaster for the arrogant, and the fall of haughty people can be part of the favor God gives to the humble. Vengeance belongs to God (see Deut 32:35; Rom 12:19; Heb 10:30), and humble people can find some comfort and satisfaction knowing that God fights for us. Godly humility will be rewarded in the end.

Enduring in Practice

For three decades I have had the pastoral privilege of coming alongside people at some of their saddest as well as most joyous moments. Like most pastors, I've officiated weddings, performed baptisms and baby dedications, and also visited hospital rooms and presided over funerals. Ministers of the gospel have the honor of hearing people confess their weaknesses, share their hopes and dreams, and lament their losses. Our task as servants of God is to help people recognize God within the ups and downs of life. Some will ask, "Where is God?" We pastors try to respond, "Right here." We want our sisters and brothers to know that God is not distant but is "a very present help in trouble" (Ps 46:1).

Humility, according to New Testament writings such as James and 1 Peter, compels us to turn toward God—not away—in times of crisis. Embodied humility enables us to discern the presence of God whether undergoing personal struggles or corporate catastrophes. During the Covid-19 pandemic, some pastors posted on social media that seminary did not prepare them to handle such a disaster. Some of the posts seemed facetious, in a misery-loves-company sort of way, but there was a sobering element to the pastors' laments. My response has been that my seminary teaching may not have informed pastors on how to handle a pandemic, but I hopefully taught them how to handle themselves regardless of the circumstances. Humility keeps our spiritual eyes open for God's presence in the bright light of day and also when darkness envelopes us.

We can find God's presence during hardships in ways that the biblical writers did not envision but nevertheless prepared us for. The New Testament's emphasis on humility urges us to draw closer to the Lord who beckons us near, especially during our most painful experiences. As we struggle to survive setbacks, failures, injustice, or any number of calamities, embodied humility brings us to God. We learn to submit to God's upright character as we pursue greater intimacy with God.

Prayer, of course, is part of this intimacy. Yet, through humility, we might also find that contemporary therapeutic practices are life-affirming and can revive the soul in troubling times. The New Testament is not a manual of contemporary psychotherapy, but it does provide a rationale for using current resources for healthier minds and bodies. Exercises, such as those associated with cognitive behavioral therapy, can help us find God's presence in the midst of our pain. Therapy does not diminish the priority of prayer; rather, our life of prayer is enhanced as we learn more about ourselves. It's a bit like Paul's words in Philippians 4:4-9. The apostle's commands for rejoicing (Phil 4:4) and to reject anxiety (Phil 4:6) occur alongside his call for prayer, thankfulness, mental reflection on wholesome ideas, and the performance of positive acts (Phil 4:6-9). His advice is sound, but not easy. Many people read the words of Philippians 4:4-9 and are encouraged by them, but cannot put those words into practice. Therapy can help us to do precisely what Paul calls for—to be prayerful, thankful, and mindful, rejecting anxiety while embracing joy.

Humility helps us to endure hardships because we look inward and upward. Looking upward means we turn to God and remember that God is love (1 Jn 4:8). Love will lead us through the difficult times. I recall making several visits to a dear sister in Christ whose body rapidly deteriorated because of ALS (amyotrophic lateral sclerosis, also known as Lou Gehrig's disease). We prayed for healing, of course, and witnessed how love sustained her even as her physical life slipped away. This sister's embodied humility kept her looking upward, seeing God's presence, even as death drew near. All who testified at her memorial service acknowledged her consistent faith and were fortified by it.

Not only do we gaze upward, we eventually look inward to see if there is anything that needs to change or grow in our attitudes and actions. The word of God speaks to us, and through humility we receive and respond to God's voice with obedience, relying on the Holy Spirit to fill and empower us as we negotiate hardships.

Not all suffering ends the way we'd like, but it does end. Deliverance takes different forms. Consider Hannah in 1 Samuel 2–3. Although Hannah was humiliated by a rival who mocked her barrenness, she humbly relied on God. Her song, 1 Samuel 2:1-10, which serves as background for Mary's song in Luke 1:46-55, not only demonstrates Hannah's resilience but also serves as a framework for much of the book of 1 Samuel. Part of her song includes these words:

> Talk no more so very proudly,
>   let not arrogance come from your mouth;

for the Lord is a God of knowledge,
  and by him actions are weighed.
The bows of the mighty are broken,
  but the feeble gird on strength.
Those who were full have hired themselves out for bread,
  but those who were hungry are fat with spoil.
The barren has borne seven,
  but she who has many children is forlorn.
The Lord kills and brings to life;
  he brings down to Sheol and raises up.
The Lord makes poor and makes rich;
  he brings low, he also exalts.
He raises up the poor from the dust;
  he lifts the needy from the ash heap,
to make them sit with princes
  and inherit a seat of honor.
For the pillars of the earth are the Lord's,
  and on them he has set the world. (1 Sam 2:3-8)

Commentator P. Kyle McCarter Jr. commends Hannah's song, saying, "These verses with the meditation upon the exaltation of the meek find the heart of the Samuel stories with singular directness. We are about to hear of the elevation of Samuel, of David—indeed even of Israel herself—from humble circumstances to power and distinction. The Song of Hannah sounds a clear keynote for what follows."[15] Hannah's deliverance comes not only through her son Samuel but also through the respect she receives as an enduring example of faithfulness. With humility we may not find the solution to the problem of pain, but we do find God, whose favor toward the humble takes manifold forms.

[15]P. Kyle McCarter Jr., *I Samuel: A New Translation*, Anchor Bible 8 (Garden City, NY: Doubleday, 1980), 76.

While we assert that God gives grace to the humble, we also confess that favor seems too frequently absent because we do not see victims vindicated. The wicked flourish and God's opposition to them seems nonexistent. In fact, there have been, and continue to be, evildoers who claim to have God on their side while they act as instruments of injustice. Proverbs 3:34 and its echoes in the Apocrypha, New Testament, and subsequent Christian literature sometimes hit us like a cruel joke because the humble get trampled by the arrogant. We must, however, understand Proverbs 3:34 as expressing the way things *are* even if not the way things *appear*. This is to say that, as is the case with all Scripture, we need to have a comprehensive—eschatological—view. Scripture's teachings play out in this life, but also in the life to come.

I have consistently been amazed at the eschatological view of many of our forebearers in the faith. I find the strength and resilience of humble people to be remarkable, especially when I recall years of testimonies of my elders in various churches. These godly people faced personal as well as societal trauma and still managed to sing, shout, and otherwise testify of the goodness and nearness of God. Sometimes we get to see the arrogant receive their comeuppance and the marginalized exalted: Davids beat their Goliaths in full view of everyone. There are times we get the job or the promotion and the self-centered colleague gets demoted or fired. But it seems more often than not that the divine reversal of Proverbs 3:34 and similar passages serves as a promise of ultimate but not present judgment.

The first readers of 1 Peter did not know how long the "little while" (1 Pet 1:6) of their trials would last, but their embodied humility assured them of God's favor. Assurance of eternal favor requires faith, and such faith will be rewarded. As we await our final reward, humility shepherds us to become wholehearted worshipers of God, experiencing God's comforting presence each day.

Chapter Seven

Worshiping

Glorifying God with Our Whole Selves

To him we offer, on the altar of the heart, the sacrifice of humility and praise, kindled by the fire of love.

Augustine

Few things are surer to cause frustration, anger, and resentment in Christian community than public worship services, especially when it comes to the style and selection of music. It's easy to think that our own preferred or familiar practices are the best. The following anonymous anecdote about the differences between hymns and praise choruses got lots of traction a couple decades or so ago:

> An old farmer went to the city one weekend and attended the big city church. He came home and his wife asked him how it was. "Well," said the farmer. "It was good. They did something different, however. They sang praise choruses instead of hymns." "Praise choruses?" asked the wife. "What are those?" "Oh, they're okay. They're sort of like hymns, only

---

Augustine, *The City of God (De Civitate Dei)*, intro. and trans. by William Babcock (Hyde Park, NY: New City Press, 1990), 308.

different," said the farmer. "Well, what's the difference?" asked the wife. The farmer said, "Well it's like this . . . If I were to say to you, 'Martha, the cows are in the corn,' well that would be a hymn. If, on the other hand, I were to say to you, 'Martha, Martha, Martha, Oh, Martha, MARTHA, MARTHA, the cows, the big cows, the brown cows, the black cows, the white cows, the black and white cows, the COWS, COWS, COWS are in the corn, are in the corn, are in the corn, in the CORN, CORN, CORN, COOOOORRRRRNNNNN,' then, if I were to repeat the whole thing two or three times, well that would be a praise chorus."

As it turns out, the exact same Sunday a young, new Christian from the city church attended the small-town church. He came home and his wife asked him how it was. "Well," said the young man, "It was good. They did something different, however. They sang hymns instead of regular songs." "Hymns?" asked the wife. "What are those?" "They're okay. They're sort of like regular songs, only different," said the young man. "Well, what's the difference?" asked the wife. The young man said, "Well it's like this . . . If I were to say to you, 'Martha, the cows are in the corn,' well that would be a regular song. If on the other hand I were to say to you,

> Oh Martha, dear Martha, hear thou my cry
> Inclinest thine ear to the words of my mouth.
> Turn thou thy whole wondrous ear by and by
> To the righteous, glorious truth.
>
> For the way of the animals who can explain
> There in their heads is no shadow of sense,
> Hearkenest they in God's sun or his rain
> Unless from the mild, tempting corn they are fenced.

Yea those cows in glad bovine, rebellious delight,
Have broke free their shackles, their warm pens eschewed.
Then goaded by minions of darkness and night
They all my mild Chilliwack sweet corn chewed.

So look to that bright shining day by and by,
Where all foul corruptions of earth are reborn
Where no vicious animal makes my soul cry
And I no longer see those foul cows in the corn.

Then, if I were to do only verses one, three and four, and change keys on the last verse, well that would be a hymn."[1]

Many regular churchgoers laugh at that anecdote because we can relate to its stereotypical take on Christian music. But worship is more than a public church service and certainly more than singing. However, in many US churches, worship means singing.

In addition to having been a pastor, I'm also an amateur musician (playing woodwinds, mostly flute and saxophone) who has been good enough to play in church for most of my life. Consequently, I've participated in more worship planning sessions than I could possibly count. I still sometimes cringe when I hear the plan to worship for a particular number of minutes, knowing that only singing is in view. However, I don't intend to be like Waldorf and Statler, the two grumpy old puppets seated in the balcony on *The Muppet Show*. Their schtick involved sarcastic comments aimed at nearly every act on *The Muppet Show* stage. I imagine that when older people complain about worship services it can come off like those balcony critics. I've always been tempted to evaluate every service for what could be better

[1] A few versions of this joke are in the public domain, but see David Packer, "The Cows Are in the Corn," *Medium*, November 15, 2009, https://medium.com/nighttimethoughts/the-cows-are-in-the-corn-8b67779ab21a, for his take on the history of the joke.

(whether I served in a visible role or not). After all, it's easy to point at church dysfunctions and to be smug about popular church practices.

Still, popular, well-attended churches invite imitation. Copying them is tempting and might be pragmatic. But humility calls us to focus on the Lord Jesus Christ and the sisters and brothers among us more than on the apparent success of other churches or on personal preferences. Biblical humility clarifies worship.

Humility summons us to self-examination so that we are continuously mindful that God is the object of worship, and God's centrality transcends any particular gathering for worship. Humble worship is redundant because it is impossible to worship apart from humility. All who worship must submit to God, which is the posture that defines humility. As Eugene Peterson writes, "Worship is the strategy by which we interrupt our preoccupation with ourselves and attend to the presence of God."[2]

While worship rightly brings us to focus on God, it does not blind us to other humans or even to ourselves. As we draw near to God, our self-perception is clarified; we own our strengths, confess our weakness, and resolve to follow Christ wholeheartedly. Worship helps us to love our neighbors because we give increasing attention to their needs and concerns. Worship is intended to describe a way of life, not a moment in time, and is not merely songs and styles of music or the performance of rituals. Worship means ascribing worth to God, and we do that by living in a manner that authenticates our profession of faith in Jesus. Our worship lifestyle extends beyond corporate gatherings, even though those gatherings are important. Yet, as meaningful as those celebratory communal times are, they represent only a portion of what it

[2]Eugene Peterson, *Leap Over a Wall: Earthy Spirituality for Everyday Christians* (New York: HarperCollins, 1997), 152.

means to worship.[3] Continual devotion to God, embodied humility, is what makes us worshipers, as the apostle Paul instructs in Romans 12.

Handing Ourselves Over to God

In my discussion of managing conflict in chapter four, I referred to Romans 12:3, 16. Those explicit references to humility, and the other ethical teachings of the last chapters of Romans, are instigated by Paul's admonition in Romans 12:1-2:

> I appeal to you therefore, brothers and sisters, by the mercies of God, to present your bodies as a living sacrifice, holy and acceptable to God, which is your spiritual worship. Do not be conformed to this world, but be transformed by the renewing of your minds, so that you may discern what is the will of God—what is good and acceptable and perfect.

The term "living sacrifice" sounds like an oxymoron when we recall that ancient Israel offered uprooted plants and slaughtered animals as part of their worship. Paul's ironic twist on Israel's practice graphically communicates what has always been true: God is pleased with our full devotion over the offering of plants, animals, money, or anything else. Isaiah 58, for example, redefines fasting as primarily the passionate pursuit of justice rather than a religious practice of devotion. The clarion call of the eighth-century-BCE prophets Amos and Micah are among the most memorable expressions of God's concern for what constitutes genuine worship.

For Amos, true worship does not involve extravagant material offerings, but the outpouring of justice and righteousness.

[3]The Covid-19 pandemic forced many churches to suspend in-person gatherings. My following discussion of sitting, eating, reading, and singing points to some of the typical aspects of Christian worship that many of us missed. While prohibited from being geographically near to fellow churchgoers, we strived to connect electronically, and our various attempts serve to highlight our need to be physically close to our faith community.

I hate, I despise your festivals,
and I take no delight in your solemn assemblies.
Even though you offer me your burnt offerings and grain offerings,
I will not accept them;
and the offerings of well-being of your fatted animals
I will not look upon.
Take away from me the noise of your songs;
I will not listen to the melody of your harps.
But let justice roll down like waters,
and righteousness like an ever-flowing stream.
(Amos 5:21-24)

The same can be said for Micah, who decries "thousands of rams, with ten thousands of rivers of oil" (Mic 6:7). In fact, God rejects material offerings in the absence of justice and righteousness. Paul's admonition in Romans 12:1-2 carries the same notions as Isaiah, Amos, and Micah. Worship, according to Paul, is not primarily the presentation of material offerings, but is foremost the handing over of our whole selves to God.

The verb "present" (*paristēmi*) in Romans 12:1 means intentionally becoming available for God's use.[4] In Romans, *paristēmi* has the sense of being at someone's disposal (e.g., Rom 6:13, 19).[5] In essence, Paul says, "hand over yourselves as sacrifices."[6] Handing over our lives—putting our entire bodies at God's disposal—is what humility entails and reinforces the point that biblical humility begins as submission to God. Worship, an outworking of humility, involves our entire being, signified by Paul's

[4]E.g., Mt 26:53, where *paristēmi* describes the readiness of angels should Jesus request their presence.
[5]See Joseph A. Fitzmyer, *Romans: A New Translation with Introduction and Commentary*, Anchor Bible 33 (New York: Doubleday, 1993), 639.
[6]James D. G. Dunn, *Romans 9–16*, Word Biblical Commentary 38B (Dallas: Word, 1988), 716.

use of the word "bodies."[7] Our bodies worship God to the degree we humbly submit to God's transformation, described here as nonconformity and mental renewal.

"The world" for Paul and other New Testament writers such as John (e.g., Jn 3:16; 1 Jn 2:15) is often shorthand for the evil and transitory nature of life in opposition to God. Scot McKnight elaborates on Paul's understanding of world in this context: "For the Romans, it especially means the way of the empire: of embattled competition for honor and status and glory, of idolatries formed in the dust of suppressing knowledge of God as Creator, of sexual indulgence outside the Creator's norms, of rebellion against Roman authorities, and most especially of any life that is not determined by love."[8] Nonconformity to the world's patterns requires mental renewal, a change of thinking, which is related to terminology regarding the mind that I've observed elsewhere (e.g., Rom 12:3, 16; Phil 2:2, 5).[9] Nonconformity also involves renouncing idols, including the idol of social status. Transformation comes about through allegiance to Christ. Allegiance is a dimension of humility because it recognizes the Lord's ultimate authority.

We display allegiance to the Lord Jesus through embodied humility, submitting our will to God's will. We discover that God's will includes love for our neighbors, particularly those we call sisters and brothers in Christ. In fact, Paul's urging in Romans 12:1-2 is directly followed by specific instructions for being living sacrifices within a community of Christ followers (especially in Rom 12:3-8). Love of God has always meant love for fellow human beings. Humility starts as submission to God and is demonstrated

---

[7]Dunn, *Romans 9–16*, 709. Scot McKnight, *Reading Romans Backwards: A Gospel of Peace in the Midst of Empire* (Waco, TX: Baylor University Press, 2019), 29-31, refers to the message of Rom 12:1-2 as "embodied sacrifice."

[8]McKnight, *Reading Romans Backwards*, 30.

[9]Paul does not use *phronēsis* terminology in Rom 12:2 but refers to *nous* (mind). See Eve-Marie Becker, *Paul on Humility*, trans. Wayne Coppins, Baylor–Mohr Siebeck Studies in Early Christianity (Waco, TX: Baylor University Press, 2020), 78-79, for the "noetic aspect of *phronesis*" in Paul, especially Philippians.

through the interactions Christians have with each other. Worship is a way of life, and it includes demonstrating total devotion to God evidenced by the way we relate to other believers.

Sitting Together

Even though worship is about more than public gatherings, the New Testament also addresses the way humility should operate in our worship services.

Perhaps you've noticed how common it is for church attendees to avoid the front few rows of the meeting place. Pastors and other church workers—especially ushers—surely have their share of stories about what appears to be a universal fear of the front seats—and especially on the part of the regular attendees. Compounding the problem of front-seat-avoidance is the reality that newcomers are left to fill the seats closest to the front, a place where they are sure to feel uncomfortable, scrutinized for their unfamiliarity with the church's liturgy.

Another issue is the tendency of some members to sit in regular seats even when it means making visitors feel unwelcome. My wife and I once visited a church that had pews—long benches that could sit at least a dozen people. When we arrived, few people were already seated, but they were mostly at the ends of the benches. My wife and I chose a row, and rather than an end-sitter scooting over to let us in, she steadfastly remained seated, forcing us to either find a different row or to somehow squeeze past her lap. Her unwillingness to accommodate us sent the message that visitors were not welcome—at least not in her row! Something as mundane as sitting can be an opportunity for regular church attendees to exercise humility.

Early Christians gathered in ways consistent with the synagogue practices of Jews in the Second Temple period.[10] James even uses

[10]See David A. deSilva, *An Introduction to the New Testament: Contexts, Methods & Ministry Formation* (Downers Grove, IL: IVP Academic, 2018), 50-51.

the term *synagōgē* when teaching a lesson about bigotry to early Jesus followers in James 2:1-4. He describes a situation that seems fanciful to some people but rings true to marginalized people:[11]

> My brothers and sisters, do you with your acts of favoritism really believe in our glorious Lord Jesus Christ? For if a person with gold rings and in fine clothes comes into your assembly, and if a poor person in dirty clothes also comes in, and if you take notice of the one wearing the fine clothes and say, "Have a seat here, please," while to the one who is poor you say, "Stand there," or, "Sit at my feet," have you not made distinctions among yourselves, and become judges with evil thoughts?

The scene likely plays out during the community's worship gathering. Manner of dress in ancient times indicated social status, as it often does today.[12] The scenario clearly illustrates classism as a rich man, bedecked in gold and "bright" clothing, is offered a seat, likely in a place where he can be noticed by the entire community. At the same time, however, an impoverished person is dishonored, instructed to stand or to sit by someone's feet. James indicts the church for becoming "judges with evil thoughts" when they show favoritism to the wealthy man while discriminating against the impoverished person. To complicate matters, the first readers of James's letter were themselves part of society's lower echelon. McKnight asserts, "Ironically, however, the poor messianic community treats one of their own with contempt while treating those who oppress them with respect—which is why James erupts as he does in 2:1, 5-7."[13]

---

[11]Some scholars have suggested James constructs a scenario for its rhetorical effect rather than describing a specific instance of which he is aware. See Luke Timothy Johnson, *The Letter of James: A New Translation with Introduction and Commentary*, Anchor Bible 37A (New York: Doubleday, 1995), 227.

[12]Scot McKnight, *The Letter of James*, New International Commentary on the New Testament (Grand Rapids, MI: Eerdmans, 2011), 183-84.

[13]McKnight, *James*, 185.

The prejudice illustrated in James 2:1-4 can become so ingrained that it develops into a system in which the rich expect to be elevated and lauded and the impoverished are expected to be satisfied with their marginal status. Hellenistic society operated with an emphasis on honor and status, but the Jesus movement had to behave differently than competitive Romans. The United States' competitive society has systematized the type of judgment that James describes. Racism and sexism, for example, are so ingrained that those in power interpret demands for equality as anarchy. It is hard for the rich to see themselves as equal to those who are economically poor and, as appears to be the case in James, it can be hard for the economically poor to feel dignified.

Humility is the remedy for correcting injustice within Christian community. Humility requires the high-minded to come down and the lowly to look up. James expects that his readers would open their eyes to the injustice perpetrated by the wealthy (e.g., Jas 2:5-7) and pursue the "royal law" of love (Jas 2:8-9). Humility rebukes the competitive character of the broader society and instead practices love. Love, as James points out, will not devalue or dehumanize the vulnerable. In fact, "religion that is pure and undefiled before God, the Father, is this: to care for orphans and widows in their distress, and to keep oneself unstained by the world" (Jas 1:27). Pure religion will not allow society's vulnerable people to remain helpless. Humility means centering the marginalized. In the context of a worshiping community, humility is submission to God, which brings our loving focus—not judgmental scrutiny—onto the most vulnerable among us.

Eating Together

Potlucks are a cultural phenomenon and appear to reflect regional and economic perspectives. For example, for several months I attended a church in West Virginia where the luck part of potluck was taken seriously and made for great fun, according to many of the members.[14] Several people gleefully recounted times when all the voluntary contributions consisted of some type of chicken dish: fried, baked, salad, and so on. Another anecdote I heard more than once was about the time when all the dishes were desserts—not one main dish arrived that evening! By contrast, I've been in churches where the people in charge of potlucks made it their responsibility to provide balanced meals and to leave nothing to chance. The luck was replaced with surety, as every attendee was assigned a type of dish to bring. Yet, in other churches where I've been pastor, several people expressed subtle—and at times overt—distrust in the quality of food coming from various unexamined kitchens. These people requested catered meals, preferring to contribute money rather than a dish to pass.

Regardless of how it gets carried out, Christians have always eaten together (see Acts 2:46). People who worship together share meals as part of their communal experience. Cultures that developed around the Mediterranean Sea are among those who have valued hospitality—including table fellowship—for eons. Christian hospitality contributed to the reputation that God's people addressed the needs of the impoverished and other vulnerable members of society.[15]

Table fellowship, however, can highlight divisions, as noted in my discussion in chapter four of Galatian conflict. I also noted that the Corinthian Christians experienced conflict related to social status: humility meant giving greater honor to those members deemed inferior. Paul addresses the Corinthians' problems around table fellowship in the context of worship gatherings, so I return

[14]I'll not mention the churches that consider "luck" to be evil and consequently refer to these meals as *potblessing* rather than *potluck*.

[15]Christine D. Pohl, *Making Room: Recovering Hospitality as a Christian Tradition* (Grand Rapids, MI: Eerdmans, 1999), 6.

to 1 Corinthians. In 1 Corinthians 11:17-22, prior to focusing on the Eucharist (1 Cor 11:23-34), Paul expresses his concerns over the way table fellowship serves to foster divisions rather than heal them. Joseph Fitzmyer writes, "Real table fellowship is lost through the inequality expressed . . . and individual selfishness causes further social divisions and factions, neglect of the poor, those whom Paul calls 'have-nots' (v. 22)."[16] Table fellowship is intimate and can help bond sisters and brothers together, so humility must reign in these worship-related gatherings as well.

One of the problems in Corinth is that those of greater social status go ahead of others, eating and drinking but not sharing. Divisions are exacerbated as some get filled and drunk while others go hungry. Paul accuses those with greater resources of humiliating, or shaming, those with fewer resources. Humility is the solution to the inequity problem because it strives to build community. Humility does not humiliate; instead it lifts up the vulnerable in the way Christ exemplified. Carla Swafford Works points out that "it is clear that some of the abuses of the Lord's Table are related to resources. In 1 Corinthians 11:17-22, some have food and drink, and others go hungry."[17] Works also realizes that humility is the solution: "Rather than preserve the social distinctions of their world, the gathering of believers should model Christ's willingness to set aside his status for the sake of another's well-being (Phil 2:5-11). Welcoming one another (11:33) implies receiving even those who have nothing, as though showing hospitality to a friend."[18]

Embodied humility appears even at potlucks, which are crucial for the formation of genuine community. I realize that some in

[16]Joseph A. Fitzmyer, *First Corinthians: A New Translation with Introduction and Commentary*, Anchor Bible 32 (New Haven, CT: Yale University Press, 2008), 435.

[17]Carla Swafford Works, *The Least of These: Paul and the Marginalized* (Grand Rapids, MI: Eerdmans, 2019), 24.

[18]Works, *Least of These*, 24.

our time might dispute the high value I just placed on table fellowship, calling it crucial. My experience, however, has continually shown that meal sharing among church members—in large as well as small numbers—is invaluable for establishing mutually beneficial relationships that can withstand a variety of threats to unity.

Reading Together

Within his discussion of Luke's account of Jesus visiting the synagogue in his hometown (Lk 4:16-30), Brian J. Wright contends that "just mentioning a Jewish assembly at a synagogue is enough to point to an opportunity for a communal reading event, since it is safe to assume that Jewish synagogue services included the reading of Scripture, whether or not Jesus would have performed such a task on each and any occasion he attended."[19] Scholars debate how prevalent private, silent, reading might have been in the ancient world, but agree that reading aloud was common.[20] Christian worship services, with synagogue practices setting precedent, included reading Scripture aloud for the entire community.

Indeed, 1 Timothy 4:13 includes the command, "Give attention to the public reading of scripture." Behind the NRSV's "give attention" is the Greek verb *prosechō*, which suggests devotion, or careful effort and not mere casual concern. While *prosechō* can carry the weight of a warning, as in Matthew and Luke (e.g., Mt 6:1; 7:15; 10:17; Lk 12:1; 17:3), it can also describe attentiveness, as with Lydia's posture toward Paul in Acts 16:14: "The Lord opened her heart to listen eagerly to what was said by Paul." According to 1 Timothy 4:13, special effort must be devoted to ensuring that the Scriptures get read, and that effort might relate to the manner of

[19]Brian J. Wright, *Communal Reading in the Time of Jesus: A Window into Early Christian Reading Practices* (Minneapolis, MN: Fortress, 2017), 129.

[20]Frank D. Gilliard, "More Silent Reading in Antiquity: *Non Omne Verbum Sonabat*," *Journal of Biblical Literature* 112, no. 4 (1993): 689-94.

reading as well as the event itself. Since public reading was necessary and expected, it needed to be done well so that listeners, who did not have written documents in hand (and may not have been literate anyway), could receive what they heard.

Humility factors into this notion of public reading because our values are reflected in how we treat the Scriptures. Since humility starts with yielding to God, and the Bible is God's Word, then we ought to make Bible reading prominent in our public gatherings. When reading is omitted or minimized, people might mistakenly view the preacher as possessing greater authority than the God of the Bible. Peter commands that people with the charism for preaching do so as if communicating the very oracles of God (1 Pet 4:11). Preachers can help draw people to God's oracles through their public speaking, which ought to accompany public reading of Scripture. However, I've noticed that in some churches, including ones that I served or simply visited, the public reading of Scripture is either abandoned or relegated to a brief passage often read by the preacher.

Churches run the risk of making the Scriptures appear superfluous and making listening seem tedious when they skip the public reading or do it poorly. Fleming Rutledge comments about her years of experience and observation regarding public Bible reading.[21] She reflects on her Grace Church congregation in New York City, which included many stage actors who could perform the Scriptures. Yet in doing so, more attention was drawn to the reader than to the text.

Rutledge passed on advice to these actors—whom she describes as expert in their ability to take direction—that she herself had received during her academic studies. Dietrich Bonhoeffer's

[21]Fleming Rutledge, "Reading the Bible in Worship for the Renewal of the Church," *Generous Orthodoxy*, September 8, 2021, https://generousorthodoxy.org/rumination/reading-the-bible-in-worship-for-the-renewal-of-the-church.

book *Life Together* gave Rutledge wisdom regarding the public reading of the Bible that she incorporated for herself and taught to others. Bonhoeffer acknowledged the difficulty of reading the Bible publicly without drawing too much attention to oneself. Rutledge quotes Bonhoeffer's admonition that "it is not easy to read the Bible aloud for others. The more artless, the more objective, the more humble one's attitude toward the material is, the better will the reading accord with the subject."[22] Rutledge and Bonhoeffer seem to suggest that the way we read the Bible in public can communicate our attitude toward God and demonstrate the way we might be evaluating others. We disrespect listeners whenever our public reading lacks care and becomes distracting rather than helpful. When we humbly prepare by practicing our reading and submitting ourselves to the needs of the community as well as to the tone of the passage, we honor God and God's people.

Singing Together

I purposely delayed the discussion of singing in an effort to counter the tendency to treat it first whenever we think of worship. There are many aspects to worship, including making financial contributions, which I'll treat in the next chapter. Worship starts with handing over our bodies to God. Worship also influences how we welcome others into our personal lives and into the life of the church. And of course, it also includes singing.

I'm not so naive as to think I'll settle debates surrounding music in church, but Paul's words in Colossians 3 might help us to exercise humility even when it comes to singing. After Paul has listed humility as one of the traits needed for community-building (Col 3:12; see chapter four), he goes on to say, "Let the word of

---

[22]Dietrich Bonhoeffer, *Life Together: The Classic Exploration of Christian Community*, trans. John W. Doberstein (San Francisco: HarperOne, 1993), 56.

Christ dwell in you richly; teach and admonish one another in all wisdom; and with gratitude in your hearts sing psalms, hymns, and spiritual songs to God" (Col 3:16). Singing is, of course, directed to God. Yet singing also is part of teaching and admonishing. McKnight goes as far as to say that Paul "envisions *catechism of one another through song*."[23]

The role of singing is related to the previous discussion of public reading. Harry Y. Gamble suggests that "the vast majority of Christians were like the larger society, illiterate, through the public reading, interpretation and exposition of texts in worship and catechesis they were strongly exposed to texts and participated in book culture to an unusual degree."[24] Catechesis required those who could read to pass on information to those who could not. Such was the case when Africans were enslaved in the Americas and preachers were among the few who could read and write. If music can be catechetical, as McKnight suggests, then it is a teaching tool whose goal is not only to glorify God but also to pass on biblical teaching to novice Christians. Humility puts our focus on the "one another" of Colossians 3:16, as our singing teaches and admonishes newer Jesus followers. The first-century context suggests that those who were literate served those who were not through singing, as with the public reading of Scripture.

In that context, however, literacy was not always an indicator of social status since enslaved people could be literate. Enslaved people handled business affairs for the paterfamilias, tutored children, and provided a range of services that required literacy.

---

[23]Scot McKnight, *The Letter to the Colossians*, New International Commentary on the New Testament (Grand Rapids, MI: Eerdmans, 2018), 331 (emphasis original).

[24]Harry Y. Gamble, "Literacy and Book Culture," in *Dictionary of New Testament Background: A Compendium of Contemporary Biblical Scholarship*, ed. Stanley E. Porter and Craig A. Evans (Downers Grove, IL: IVP Academic, 2000), 646. Wright, *Communal Reading in the Time of Jesus*, challenges some of the assumptions regarding how widespread illiteracy was in the ancient world, but nevertheless agrees that public reading was central to communal life.

The way that literate people in the early centuries might have served illiterate people is analogous to how mature Christians today might serve those who are less experienced. For example, the selection and style of music should acknowledge the needs of those who are newer to Christian faith, who are being catechized, as it were. When we craft corporate services, we ought to have in mind those less familiar with the Bible, theological ideas, and Christian practices.

Music has a wide range of influence, from setting an emotional tone to signaling various movements within a worship service. However, humility reminds us of music's catechetical function, encouraging us to always keep in mind those who are following us on the journey of faith. Unfortunately, congregational singing can also be a way for some Christians to assert their social dominance. Song selections typically reflect the preferences of the dominant culture or of the long-standing church members, but humility requires moving out of comfortable, well-worn patterns, and discerning the needs—not just stylistic tastes—of the minoritized and newer Jesus followers.

Humble Worship in Practice

For just over six years I served in pastoral roles at a prominent urban church. The church was predominantly White even though the city was mostly Black.

The church had always experienced people knocking on the door or ringing the bell during weekdays, requesting cash, and as might be expected, many of those people were Black. Urban churches continually struggle with how best to respond to random requests for food, transportation fare, or money for any variety of needs. This church's challenges were complicated because of the racial dynamics often involved. We who worked in the office understandably grew weary of the random knocks and doorbell rings, but sometimes fellow staff members could not hide their frustration and began to make judgments based on appearances, even on the day they met my father.

My father, along with his new wife whom he married many years after my mother passed away, stopped to visit me and my family. This couple in their early seventies were dressed casually, as might be expected of those on a road trip. I excitedly walked with them from my house to the church building, eager for them to see the sanctuary and my office.

As we climbed the stairs to my office, we had to pass the secretary, who, on seeing my father and stepmother, dropped her head and averted her eyes as if to avoid dealing with yet another needy person. I ignored her but had to pass by another staff member's office. I decided to introduce my folks to this person, but when they responded to my knock and invited me in, they immediately sighed, removed their glasses, and lowered their head, apparently dreading an encounter with a needy family. I announced, "This is my father," and immediately this staff person's countenance changed. They raised their head, got out of their seat, and greeted my father and stepmother. It was awkward.

When we left to head back to my house, my father asked, "Does [that staff member] have any Black friends?" Because I was brand new to the church, I did all I could to defend my fellow staff member as well as my decision to work there. It did not take long, however, for me to see the extent to which humility was lacking among members of the leadership of that congregation and how that lack affected ministry to the church's neighbors. My wife and I ministered to Black people of modest means who lived within walking distance of the church, often having them in our home. Almost every person told us directly that they did not feel welcome among our congregation because of the racial makeup as well as the emphasis on social status and formal education.

Some churches spend exorbitant amounts of money on accoutrements associated with Christian worship: sound systems, projectors, screens, smoke machines, cushioned stadium seating, and so much more. None of that is evil, of course, but those practical items are meaningless (maybe especially the smoke machine) without embodied humility.

That prejudiced treatment of my father and stepmother is locked in my memory, so I am determined to embody humility and welcome even strangers, while hoping that I can encourage such a perspective wherever I serve. “Welcoming the stranger” was one of the stated core values of the church I planted after resigning from that aforementioned church. Our new church started out of my home in a neighborhood where many in poverty lived within blocks of those with plenty. Opulent homes were a short walk from public housing units, and our church sought to bridge societal chasms of race, sex, and socioeconomic status. I recollect fondly people whose paths would likely never have intersected if not for our church. Peace Fellowship Church in Washington, DC, continues to be a community that embodies humility, demonstrating that worshiping Jesus is not confined to the public Sunday gathering but encompasses all of life. Humility must guide our efforts in the management of all that God gives us, which is the practice of stewardship.

Chapter Eight

Stewarding

Attitude More Than Obligation

You shall not exalt yourself, but shall be humble-minded in every respect. You shall not claim glory for yourself. You shall not hatch evil plots against your neighbor. You shall not permit your soul to become arrogant.

THE EPISTLE OF BARNABAS 19.3

MAYBE YOU HAVE BEEN PRESENT FOR THE passionate request for money that serves as an event's emotionally charged finale. After the pragmatic presentation of some not-for-profit organization's mission, its current services, and its future hopes, a charismatic speaker takes center stage to make an appeal for financial contributions. Some of the hundreds—possibly thousands—of public appeals for money that I've witnessed in churches, on television, and in various other gatherings were protracted and manipulative spectacles aiming to shame attendees into giving.

My wife and I were flabbergasted at a large urban church's unsettling collection of the offering during our visit to one of their

From Michael W. Holmes, trans., *The Apostolic Fathers: Greek Texts and English Translations*, 2nd ed. (Grand Rapids, MI: Baker Books, 1999).

Sunday services. At one point in the program, a bejeweled pastor wearing designer clothes demanded that those possessing the designated envelopes containing their tithes stand up, turn to those seated—the people without envelopes—and ask why they were not tithing. The envelope-bearers, along with others who happened to be contributing money without envelopes, were then directed to process around the front of the auditorium in order to deposit their donations. After hundreds of people put money in the collection baskets, the pastor returned to the podium. She went on to demand that the church needed more money and we attendees needed to dig deeper and make additional contributions immediately—even though there had been no way the money could have already been counted.

The church's website stated that typically worship services were around ninety minutes long, but the offering drama that day had taken so much time that the service was close to the ninety-minute mark when my wife and I left. The scheduled sermon had not even been given yet. Not only was the hour getting late and we had other engagements, we frankly found the unscheduled appeal for money to be off-putting.

I have many times witnessed events like what happened at that church, and it has never sat well with me. Consequently, during my years of pastoral ministry, I never made aggressive demands for money. Yet some of my fellow church attendees assumed my lack of emotional financial appeals indicated I was uninterested in monetary matters. However, I have always been interested in how churches discuss and handle financial matters for the institution as well as for attendees.

In my experience, larger churches seemed to manage their finances well while small churches appeared disorganized. But those small churches were typically quicker to respond to communal crises and were obviously sacrificial in their generosity. As

I started preaching in my twenties, whenever I was a guest speaker at a relatively large church, I was thrilled to receive an honorarium. In those larger, organized congregations, my payment was typically an already-prepared check, sometimes handed to me before I preached. On many other occasions over the years, I preached in smaller churches and was similarly delighted to receive an honorarium. However, the amount of the remuneration was often surprisingly greater than that of larger churches. Those smaller churches would sometimes collect a special "speaker's offering" during the service that was as much as ten times greater than what I received in larger churches. I don't relay this anecdote as a recommendation—especially since some churches may not have been as careful about tax laws as they should have been—but simply to explain some of what contributed to my pastoral perspectives on addressing financial matters.

Early in my ministry, I developed a relaxed posture toward asking for money, confident that the Lord would provide whatever was needed. When I served larger congregations, I realized that my small-minded perspective was not usually appreciated. Church is big business, and there needs to be a strategy for acquiring and managing finances—at least that is what I started to learn. In light of the Covid-19 pandemic, Christian institutions—including churches and seminaries—are struggling more than ever to stay financially viable. Even so, our approach to finances, like all other matters, must not be driven by fear, by concerns over scarcity, or by status-seeking. As naive as it may sound, humility—as a companion of faith—must guide stewardship.

Humility and the Three Ts

I often chuckle when I hear the word *stewardship* in a Christian context because it often serves as a euphemism for contributing money, particularly tithes and offerings. That's why I opened a chapter on stewardship with anecdotes about money. Pastors preach annual stewardship sermons, or entire series of messages that address the familiar three Ts of stewardship: time, talent, and treasure. Those sermons admonish us to use our spiritual gifts, to care for God's creation, and even to maintain good physical health. The main focus, however, is typically money. We desire for *stewardship* to signify more than money—but certainly not less than it either.

Beyond noting some issues related to church finances, I want to consider stewardship more broadly, and how humility affects how we care *about* and care *for* people and things. Sermons about volunteering, using spiritual gifts, and contributing money are framed as part of the Christian obligation to share what we have been given. We are obliged, in some sense, because everything we have comes from the Lord (see Jas 1:17), but I am striving for a greater sense of altruism rather than duty when it comes to giving. Humility reveals that stewardship is to a greater degree about people rather than things. This is to say that how and why we give is more important to God than the volume of our gift.

Consider the widow (in Mk 12:42 and Lk 21:2) who donated two small copper coins to the temple treasury. Jesus commends her to the disciples for giving out of poverty, not abundance. Part of the lesson Jesus offers is that financial giving can demonstrate faith in God. The widow, who was vulnerable, with virtually no one in society on whom she could depend, presumably trusted God enough to give away all her resources. Others, however, contributed out of their abundance, indicating that their gifts were not a sacrifice and, therefore, demonstrated little faith. While part of the lesson is about faith, another part is about being humble enough to learn spiritual truth from a person who is weak, vulnerable, and easily ignored. The widow and her offering are a rebuke to arrogant donors. An impoverished Jewish widow in occupied territory gives us all a critical lesson about financial giving and faith in God.

The marginalized people that Jesus brings to our attention are the ones who teach us about humility. Such is the case when Jesus blessed children (e.g., Mk 10:13-16), or taught about neighborliness with an unexpected Samaritan hero (Lk 10:25-37). The Lord's choice of a peasant girl to bear the Messiah (Lk 1:26-38), and the divine reversal that girl sings about (Lk 1:46-55) and that is illustrated in the story of Lazarus and the rich man (Lk 16:19-31), indicate how the lowly—the humble and even the humiliated—are the ones we need to heed if we are to understand what God's kingdom is like. We tend to take our spiritual cues from prominent people, but in doing so we absorb more of society's competitive codes of conduct rather than the countercultural values of God's kingdom. Humility tells us to look past the popular people and let our eyes fall on the seemingly insignificant in order to gain spiritual wisdom for the stewardship of every area of life.

Luke rarely uses the formal language of humility that we have come to recognize and appreciate, yet he presents examples of how ordinary followers of Jesus embody humility in a variety of circumstances.[1] Many unsung heroes of the emerging Christian church appear in Luke's writings. Ananias of Damascus and Barnabas are but two examples of how humility relates to the stewardship of time, talent, and treasure.[2]

Acts 9:1-25 recounts the story of the risen Christ confronting Saul of Tarsus, who was on his way from Jerusalem to Damascus under the authority of the high priest to apprehend Jesus followers.

---

[1]The Greek work *tapeinos* in Mary's song (Lk 1:52) emphasizes divine reversal as does the verb *tapeinoō* in Lk 3:5 (allusion to the LXX of Is 40:4) and also in the axiom cautioning against self-elevation (Lk 14:11; 18:14).

[2]Luke mentions three people with the name Ananias. The first is the infamous Ananias introduced in Acts 5:1, who, being vainglorious, provides a counterexample of embodied humility as he and his wife Sapphira attempt to appear magnanimous, like Joseph called Barnabas (Acts 4:36-37). The other Ananias is the high priest mentioned in Acts 23:2; 24:1.

Saul's encounter with Jesus (Acts 9:1-9), his subsequent preaching (Acts 9:19-22), and his narrow escape from Damascus in a basket (Acts 9:23-25) tend to overshadow Ananias's role in the drama of Acts 9. However, Ananias embodies humility and is critical to Christian history.

Ananias, the unsung hero in Damascus, demonstrates how humility starts as yielding to God and moves to establish community. The risen Christ appears to Ananias in order to prepare Damascus disciples to meet the blind and disoriented Saul (Acts 9:10-12). Ananias knows Saul's reputation and expresses his concerns about meeting the zealous persecutor of Jesus followers (Acts 9:13). After all, Ananias, a Damascus disciple, is one of Saul's targets.[3] The risen Christ responds to Ananias, who moves into action, readily embracing a new disciple of Jesus Christ as part of the growing community (Acts 9:15-17). Luke uses the verb *apostellō* (I send) to indicate Ananias's divine commission.[4]

Humility is more than simply being nice; it accompanies tenacious faith, requiring personal sacrifice. With no time to observe the sincerity of Saul's faith in Jesus, Ananias takes a risk and literally reaches out, laying hands on Saul. Ananias welcomes Saul as brother, a term that is one of the apostle Paul's favorites in his letters.[5] Stewardship, as seen in the actions of Ananias, not only encompasses oversight and care but also requires an investment whose return is not guaranteed. Humility shifts our focus away from self-promotion, rejects pride and vainglory, and seeks the welfare of others. We know that our displays of love and concern are not always graciously received or reciprocated. Humility

[3]See Joseph A. Fitzmyer, *The Acts of the Apostles*, Anchor Bible 31 (New York: Doubleday, 1998), 426.

[4]Craig S. Keener, *Acts: An Exegetical Commentary*, vol. 1. (Grand Rapids, MI: Baker Academic, 2012), 1660.

[5]Fitzmyer, *Acts*, 429, observes that while "brother" could be a familiar greeting between two Jewish men, it seems more likely that Ananias welcomes Saul as a fellow disciple.

highlights how *agapē* love gives without expecting anything positive in return, recognizing that even vitriol might be the response to good works.

Ananias is an example of how humility relates to stewardship because he put the interests of the Lord and other Christians ahead of his own, using his time and risking his reputation to build the new community of believers. Ananias fades into the background of Acts, but we do well to note Paul's description of him, which are Luke's final words about Ananias: "a devout man according to the law and well spoken of by all the Jews living there" (Acts 22:12).[6] Humility welcomes a supporting role and doesn't crave the spotlight, which is perhaps why we are ambiguous about humility's value.

Our competitive society claims to value humility yet pressures us to crave being the center of attention. Some will ask, "Why can't I have it all—celebrity status and humility?" Humility, however, being more radical than we might imagine, invites us to ask, "Why *must* I have it all?" As Jesus put it, "For what will it profit them to gain the whole world and forfeit their life?" (Mk 8:36). Humility is a necessary ingredient of Christian discipleship and reorients our focus so our questions and concerns will be about obeying God, about communing with sisters and brothers, and about trusting God's grace to place us where we need to be at the right time. Ananias may not be the main character in Acts, but his positive reputation lives forever in Scripture. His devotion to God and his upright character made him the perfect choice for that critical moment of welcoming Saul of Tarsus and changing the course of history.

Another key figure in Saul's life is Barnabas. While he is more well known than Ananias, after his rift with Paul in Acts 15:36-40

[6]In the Orthodox Church, October 1 is the feast day of Ananias of Damascus. It is January 25 in the Roman Catholic, Anglican, and Lutheran Churches—the same day as the Feast of Saint Paul's Conversion. Ananias remains in the shadow of Saul of Tarsus.

he disappears from Acts, though he is mentioned in Pauline letters (e.g., 1 Cor 9:6; Gal 2:9; Col 4:10). Barnabas illustrates humility's place in stewardship in at least a couple of ways, the first being financially. Barnabas appears in Acts 4:36-37 as a prime example of how members of the burgeoning Jesus way were working to eliminate poverty by sharing possessions rather than hoarding them (Acts 4:32-35). Joseph, a Levite from Cyprus, contributed financially to the apostolic ministry, earning the nickname Barnabas, "son of encouragement," an Aramaic way of saying "encourager."

Barnabas reveals how financial stewardship goes beyond contributing money but also prioritizes generosity that flows from selfless consideration for others, as Luke's account of a different Ananias, and his wife Sapphira, illustrates. Ananias and Sapphira sold property as Barnabas had done but brought only part of the proceeds to the apostles' feet while indicating that they had contributed all of the proceeds (Acts 5:1-2). The apostle Peter's rebuke of Ananias (Acts 5:3-4) reveals that the couple's sin was not holding back money per se but dishonesty. They were vainglorious, wanting to appear more generous than they actually were. Judging from the flow of Luke's storytelling, Ananias and Sapphira wanted the same sort of recognition Barnabas received. Instead, their behavior serves as a warning since they died suddenly and publicly as a result of lying to the Holy Spirit (Acts 5:4-11). Ananias and Sapphira wanted greater status within the fledgling Christian community and, using the strategy of the broader society, attempted to purchase that status. The link between Barnabas's generosity in Acts 4:36-37 and the events of Acts 5:1-11 dramatizes the axiom explored in chapter one: "God opposes the proud but gives grace to the humble" (Jas 4:6; 1 Pet 5:5; cf. Prov 3:34).

The second way Barnabas links humility to stewardship is how he, like Ananias of Damascus, welcomes Saul and also vouches for him (Acts 9:26-27). The Jerusalem disciples were understandably frightened of Saul, who had earlier consented to the stoning of Stephen just outside of their city (Acts 7:58–8:1). According to Luke, sometime after Saul's preaching in Damascus and his dramatic escape from that city, the new apostle arrived in Jerusalem.[7] Barnabas defended Saul, managing to assuage the fears of the Jerusalem disciples. Barnabas, the encourager, embodied humility in the way he stewarded his money and his reputation.

Humility and the Stewardship of Creation

Partisan politics overshadows scientific concerns about climate change. Most scientists agree that the world's climate is changing as the planet warms, and that humans contribute significantly to this global crisis. However, there is a vocal minority that either denies climate change or recognizes it without holding humans responsible.

While climate change is one—albeit controversial—aspect of environmental concern, there are Christians who minimize or outright denounce the work of environmental justice altogether. (That word *justice* is itself enough to provoke negative reactions from some Christians.) Some Christians see biblical passages that point to the earth's destruction, such as 2 Peter 3:12, which indicates that "the heavens will be set ablaze and dissolved, and the elements will melt with fire" when the Lord returns (see also Rev 21:1), as absolving them of any responsibility to conserve the environment. In light of the earth's eventual demise, these Christians see little or no point in preserving natural resources, limiting pollutants in air and water, or treating animals more humanely. For

[7]See, e.g., Fitzmyer, *Acts*, 433, and Craig S. Keener, *Galatians: A Commentary* (Grand Rapids, MI: Baker Academic, 2018), 90-91, as examples of scholarly attempts to reconcile Luke's account of Saul's life immediately after the Damascus road incident (Acts 9:19-30) with the apostle's words in Gal 1:17–2:10, where he recounts his call from Jesus to preach the gospel as well as his trip to Arabia and visits to Jerusalem after receiving his call.

these Christians, the Genesis creation account means that human dominion over creation includes the authority to exploit the material and animal world.

On the sixth day of creation, according to Genesis 1:26-28, after God made all sorts of animals, there was more work to be done:

> Then God said, "Let us make humankind in our image, according to our likeness; and let them have dominion over the fish of the sea, and over the birds of the air, and over the cattle, and over all the wild animals of the earth, and over every creeping thing that creeps upon the earth."
>
> So God created humankind in his image,
> in the image of God he created them;
> male and female he created them.
>
> God blessed them, and God said to them, "Be fruitful and multiply, and fill the earth and subdue it; and have dominion over the fish of the sea and over the birds of the air and over every living thing that moves upon the earth."

Some Bible readers understand "dominion" as license for exploitation, but the term is meant to mirror God's rule over the entire universe. Humans, who are made in the image of God, must exercise authority over the earth in the loving way that God rules.[8] Douglas Moo and Jonathan Moo assert that human dominion is akin to God's royal reign, and "such an understanding of kingship makes impossible any interpretation of *dominion* in Genesis 1:26-28 as *domination*, and it rules out any notion that God's

[8]Victor P. Hamilton, *The Book of Genesis: Chapters 1-17*, New International Commentary on the Old Testament (Grand Rapids, MI: Eerdmans, 1990), 139-40; Douglas J. Moo and Jonathan A. Moo, *Creation Care: A Biblical Theology of the Natural World*, Biblical Theology for Life (Grand Rapids, MI: Zondervan, 2018), 76-80. See the survey of how various texts, such as Gen 1:28 and 2 Pet 3:10-12, have factored into discussions of theology and environmentalism in David G. Horrell, Cherryl Hunt, and Christopher Southgate, *Greening Paul: Rereading the Apostle in a Time of Ecological Crisis* (Waco, TX: Baylor University Press, 2010), 11-32.

entrusting of other creatures into our care means that we may use them or the rest of creation however we like."[9]

It is humility that keeps *dominion* from becoming *domination.* Humility resists exploitation and instead strives for the flourishing of God's creation—including the vegetation, animals, and inanimate resources. Humility's place in the stewardship of creation is made even more vivid with the image of a person's care for the well-being of their cattle. Proverbs 12:10 says,

> The righteous know the needs of their animals,
>   but the mercy of the wicked is cruel.

"Needs" is the Hebrew *nephesh*, which is often translated "soul," but is indicative of comprehensive well-being. The overall picture is one of compassionate concern, like that of the shepherd in Psalm 23. The righteous or just person stands in contrast to wicked people who lack the humility to care for their animals. Put bluntly and sarcastically, cruelty is the best mercy the wicked can muster.

Concerns over the treatment of animals as well as questions about the negative environmental impact of large-scale animal farming leads some people—including Christians—to vegetarianism.[10] According to *Greening Paul: Rereading the Apostle in a Time of Ecological Crisis*, some Bible readers conclude that vegetarianism is one of the best options for environmental stewardship. However, the authors, David G. Horrell, Cherryl Hunt, and Christopher Southgate conclude that Pauline texts

> have generated an eschatological narrative structure in which humans have a responsibility to express their new identity as freed, reconciled creatures in working for

---

[9]Moo and Moo, *Creation Care*, 80.

[10]See, e.g., John M. G. Barclay, "Food, Christian Identity and Global Warming: A Pauline Call for Christian Food Taboo" in *Expository Times* 121, no. 12 (2010): 585-93, and the response by Tim Gorringe, "Rise Peter! Kill and Eat: A Response to John Barclay," *Expository Times* 123, no. 2 (2011): 63-69.

> reconciliation, peace, and liberation throughout all creation. But this vision, particularly when brought into dialogue with scientific and ecological insights, might, we would argue, be better enacted in a commitment to generous and reverential patterns of human-animal relationships, to small-scale, sustainable, and locally focused agriculture rather than to vegetarianism.[11]

Vegetarianism invites vigorous debates, but it seems helpful that increasing numbers of Christians are reading the Bible with regard for the world's ongoing environmental challenges. Horrell, Hunt, and Southgate connect humility and the stewardship of creation with their discussion of ethical kenosis, or self-emptying, derived from their reading of Philippians 2:1-11.[12] These authors identify three aspects of kenosis that I associate with humility:[13]

1. Kenosis of aspiration, which resists grasping for or clinging to "a role or position, rather than willingly following obediently in God's purposes for the good of others, even when closely suffering is the result."
2. Kenosis of appetite, which resists the compulsion to "gain power over others" or succumb to idolatry, which makes "a substance or experience a kind of substitute god." This type of kenosis has particular application to the environment because idolatrous appetites lead to consuming "more of the world's fullness than is our share."
3. Kenosis of acquisitiveness, which is the desire for "the material trappings of life, which again are often acquired at the expense of the well-being of other creatures."

[11]Horrell, Hunt, and Southgate, *Greening Paul*, 202-6, responding sympathetically but challenging the views of priest and theologian Andrew Linzey, *Animal Theology* (London: SCM Press, 1994).

[12]See the discussion of kenosis in chap. 2.

[13]Horrell, Hunt, Southgate, *Greening Paul*, 198-200.

Kenosis is one way to describe humility, and these dimensions apply to all aspects of life, including our relationship to the natural world. Some might object to the notion of humility being applied to nonhuman creation, but it should be obvious that our treatment of the earth affects other human beings. Dumping waste in economically disadvantaged communities, polluting water that indigenous people depend on, or not reducing carcinogenic chemicals from factories for political reasons are examples of how a lack of environmental stewardship betrays a lack of humanitarian concern.

Human beings have increasing knowledge about how to use the earth's resources—including animals—but the question is, Do we have the humility to steward what God has created? Our humility starts as yielding to God and moves us toward establishing healthy community where we recognize our need for others. The more we realize how much we need and depend on all of God's creation, the humbler we can be about our interactions with it.

Humility and Self-Care

I was taught "the ministry is not your life; your life is your ministry." The ones who gave me this maxim had worked with burned-out Christian workers, some of whom questioned their worth and identity after leaving "the ministry." Those struggling servants had defined ministry as the specific role they filled within a church or other Christian organization, so when they could not continue in their roles, they felt disoriented—out of step with God, with others, and even with themselves.

When we recognize that ministry encompasses our entire lives, as I argued previously from Romans 12:1-2, we start integrating and not compartmentalizing. When we compartmentalize, we create hierarchies, with ranking systems that might be felt if not always expressed. For example, it was typical for pastors in the generation before me to sacrifice their families for church work by being out of the house several nights each week, by traveling to speaking engagements without their families, by continually having visitors in the home, or by requiring spouses and children to always be in attendance at church events or having them serve as unpaid workers in all church activities. For these pastors, their unexpressed ranking system put their expectations of what the church needed (particularly the concerns voiced by the most judgmental members) ahead of their own families' concerns. Perhaps in reaction to such behavior, pastors in my generation have almost turned their families into idols, with male pastors extolling the physical beauty of their wives and the unprecedented skills of their children. We all risk being sucked into the social media vortex where boasting is normalized and encouraged.

Fortunately, God has people—including some on social media who manage to inform rather than perform—who remind us of the need to be authentic and to reckon with our human limitations. Recall how Jesus got away from the daily grind for rest and prayer (e.g., Mk 1:35). In fact, Jesus practiced such self-care that he could remain asleep in a boat during a terrifying storm (Mk 4:35-41). Kirk Byron Jones, in his treatise on self-care, reflects on the Synoptic Gospels' account of Jesus in the boat: "*Three cheers for the sleeping Savior!* Of all the artistic depictions of Jesus I have seen, I do not believe I have ever seen a picture of Jesus asleep. Perhaps our perceptions of the ever-busy, ever-ready Jesus feed our own addiction to busyness."[14]

To say that "my life is my ministry" is to acknowledge that everything we do—vocationally and even recreationally—is consecrated to God. Consequently, ministry includes at least the care of my body, my mind, my family, my friends, and the earth. Self-care

[14]Kirk Byron Jones, *Rest in the Storm: Self-Care Strategies for Clergy and Other Caregivers* (Valley Forge, PA: Judson, 2001), 25 (emphasis original).

requires humility because it is pride that lurks behind workaholism. Our competitive society distorts our view of life, making us think that rest is a waste of time. Arrogance can cause Christian workers to resist rejuvenation through rest, but humility draws us back to the Shepherd who calls us to rest in green pastures, leads us to peaceful waters, and restores our souls (Ps 23:1-3).

Stewarding in Practice

I was invited to a restaurant for a lunch meeting with a wealthy Christian. He gave me a tour of his offices and recounted how he earned his wealth, making clear the amount of money he had donated over the previous few years. To be fair, he emphasized how much good his money was doing throughout the world, especially in underdeveloped countries. Over time, however, it became apparent to me that many members of his congregation were in awe of this man because of his wealth and status. While I am grateful that this person's money proved helpful in some contexts, my observations and encounters with him reinforced my belief that humility is more valuable than money.

We need money for all sorts of reasons, but we don't need to alienate sisters and brothers through the arrogance that often accompanies wealth. Stewardship is not only about what—or how much—we give away, but also about the manner in which we give. As 1 Peter 4:10-11 admonishes, our gifts are animated by God's Spirit and intended for God's glory.

Several years after that lunch meeting, I was invited to a different lunch gathering. It was only after several pleasant interactions with the host that I discovered, in a roundabout way, that he was wealthy and contributed significantly to his church—as well as to other organizations. This man was known not only for his friendliness but also for the way he mentored countless individuals, some of whom came to share his Christian faith.

The two men I mention are, of course, the products of varied familial and environmental factors, yet their wealth and Christian faith invite some degree of comparison. I don't know the financial net worth of either man, but I do know the way each made me feel in their presence as I shared meals and had other interactions with them. The first man made clear that I was constantly being evaluated, and I saw how money functioned as his calling card because it identified him and the power he wielded, even in his church. With the second man, however, I consistently felt the warmth of brotherhood that was never overshadowed by his wealth.

Money is the most obvious way we think of stewardship, but the notion applies to most of life's interactions with humans as well as the environment. Stewardship is management, and we need humility to be effective managers who keeps their attention on God and others. Humility does not emphasize what might be permissible, but rather those things that are most edifying for communal life, including the care of God's creation.

My family knows I'm a bit obsessive about recycling, preserving, and reusing in order to avoid unnecessary waste. And yes, I've driven a hybrid for seventeen years (bought a Prius after the Civic hybrid was totaled in a crash). I am also a vegetarian flirting with veganism because of environmental concerns, and I've long been a gym rat, racquetballer, and cyclist, trying to care for my body. In striving to cultivate humility, I cannot be smug about my feeble efforts because the environmental predicament and challenges to good health are too vast. Yet I am reminded that even feeble efforts matter to God, just like the widow with her two coins. Humility empowers us to be fruitful disciples of the Lord Jesus Christ and to do all we can to love God and love our neighbors.

Chapter Nine

Empowering

Power to the People Who Are Poor in Spirit

Humility has two feet: appreciation of divine power and consciousness of personal weakness.

Bernard of Clairvaux

Is it cruel to admonish the humiliated to become humbler? Should lowly people be expected to go even lower? Is it Christlike to expect the powerless of society to serve the powerful when that is precisely what they're already doing? How ought oppressed Christians respond to biblical instructions for self-emptying, or serving others, or forgiving?

In *Reading in Communion: Scripture and Ethics in Christian Life*, Stephen E. Fowl and L. Gregory Jones discuss the need for Christians to "read the Scriptures 'over against ourselves' rather than simply 'for ourselves.'"[1] According to Fowl and Jones, "Allowing ourselves to be interrogated by Scripture entails a willingness to struggle with difficult and/or obscure texts. But of course there is no *a priori* way to know what texts we will find difficult or

Cited in Jane Foulcher, *Reclaiming Humility: Four Studies in the Monastic Tradition*, Cistercian Studies 255 (Collegeville, MN: Cistercian Publications, 2015), 193.

[1]Stephen E. Fowl and L. Gregory Jones, *Reading in Communion: Scripture and Ethics in Christian Life* (Grand Rapids, MI: Eerdmans, 1991), 42-44 (quote from 42).

obscure."[2] Marginalized people cannot help but to hear or read some Scripture passages with suspicion if not wholesale rejection, especially when those passages were used to support injustices such as slavery and patriarchy.

Fowl and Jones offer South African cleric and activist Allan Boesak as an example of an oppressed Christian attempting to allow Scripture to "interrogate him" as he wondered how he could ever tell Blacks in South Africa to forgive seventy times seven (Mt 18:21-22).[3] The nuances of forgiveness are complex, and beyond my present analysis, yet Boesak's dilemma is one that marginalized people consistently grapple with and relates to the topic of humility.[4] Humility, and the concomitant notion of kenosis (see Phil 2:7), can appear to be a formula for repression and not liberation. Yielding to God and serving others seems to reinforce social caste systems rather than dismantle them. True humility, however, does not ignore or accept oppression, but instead seeks human flourishing by eliminating injustice through self-sacrificial love.

According to Stephen T. Pardue, Augustine of Hippo claimed that while "humility's primary function is to restrain and limit, it also has a secondary, empowering function. Thus, Christ's humility is not only what moves him to become incarnate and crucified (restraining), but also what allows him to live a life perfectly animated by the Spirit (empowering)."[5] The Holy Spirit provides supernatural power for perseverance and tranquility in the face of injustice, and in some cases the humble faithful are protected and vindicated in this life in the way that Shadrach, Meshach, and Abednego survived their attempted executions in a furnace

---

[2]Fowl and Jones, *Reading in Communion*, 42.

[3]Fowl and Jones, *Reading in Communion*, 43.

[4]To examine some of the complexities of forgiveness, especially with regard to injustice on a large scale, see Miroslav Volf, *The End of Memory: Remembering Rightly in a Violent World* (Grand Rapids, MI: Eerdmans, 2006).

[5]See Stephen T. Pardue, *The Mind of Christ: Humility and the Intellect in Early Christian Theology*, T&T Clark Studies in Systematic Theology 23 (London: Bloomsbury T&T Clark, 2013), 145.

(Dan 3). We must admit, however, that not all faithful followers of Jesus who suffer injustice are delivered or vindicated in their lifetimes. Consider as examples Stephen who was killed by a mob (Acts 7:54-60), the apostle James who was executed by Herod (Acts 12:1-2), and those among the host of faithful heralded in Hebrews 11 who suffered horrible injustices (Heb 11:35-38). Still, God gave them strength to the end.

Humility is both restraining and empowering because God opposes the arrogant but is gracious toward the humble. God's opposition to the arrogant means we must all learn to embrace humility or face the consequences brought on by hubris. Be humble or be humbled! The axiom of Proverbs 3:34, which reverberates throughout Scripture and later Christian writings, insists that humility restrains self-aggrandizement while stimulating dependence on the power of the Holy Spirit. The Spirit's power enables individuals and communities to become more like Christ, which means genuine love for God and for God's creation.

Humility is also empowering in that it liberates us from the bondage of society's expectations and limitations. Humble people are free to live the Jesus way, not beholden to synthetic systems that enslave, devalue, and dehumanize some people while upholding a minority of the population who bully the rest. The way of the world pressures people to become competitive, hierarchical, and power hungry, leading to the exploitation of other humans along with the natural environment. Consequently, the world vilifies humility because it appears disempowering and reinforces society's stratifications. The powerful never consider relinquishing power because they fear being dominated in the ways they have dominated others. By contrast, the powerless are destined to crave, demand, scratch, and claw for the same power that oppresses them. Humility, when regarded as limiting, weak, and passive, could never be taken seriously, and we have no imagination for how humility could be an agent of equity. We conclude that worldly power is never ceded but must be taken, which is, of course, the way the world operates, and it is naive to think there might be a better way. However, it is vital that we find a better way because the status quo is costly—human beings kill each other and deplete natural resources because we refuse to practice the countercultural Jesus way of humility.

Jesus followers are expected to rely on the Holy Spirit's power to rearrange societal patterns and dissolve abusive human tendencies so that our love for God and God's creatures provokes a new imagination. This new imagination leads to the creation of new communities and new policies that uphold human dignity. Embodying humility takes seriously our mandate to love God and to love others (e.g., Mk 12:30-31), making us more authentically human—more like Jesus Christ. Humility becomes empowering when we yield to the Holy Spirit, the One who empowers (see Acts 1:8), and when we embrace the paradoxical nature of God's kingdom, where the way up is down and the first are last (Mt 20:16).

God rewards those who practice such dependence on the Spirit's power, yet the rewards in this life are incomplete because the greatest rewards are reserved for the life yet to come. In the eschaton, the end of the age, God's divine reversal will vindicate and elevate the lowly and humiliated people. Yet in the meantime, humility's power works through the lowly, enabling them to become the best witnesses of genuine Christlikeness. God always takes what appears foolish in order to confound the wise and causes what is lowly to rebuke the alleged powerful (see 1 Cor 1:27-29). And as a foreshadowing of the eschaton, there are occasions in this age when the lowly are raised while the arrogant are taken down.

The Wealthy Poor

God works most powerfully through those whom society rejects or marginalizes.[6] That is sometimes of little consolation to those on the margins because we've been conditioned to think of humility as weakness.[7] However, God's design is to demonstrate supernatural power through human weakness. Faith allows us to experience God's power through agents who typically get pushed to the side but are rich in faith.

In chapter seven I discussed the horrendous display of favoritism presented in James 2:1-4, and now I focus on the admonition that directly follows in James 2:5: "Be attentive, my beloved sisters and brothers: Didn't God choose for himself the poor of this world—the rich in faith and heirs of the kingdom, which he promised to those who love him?" (my translation). Most translations add some form of the verb "to be" (i.e., "to be rich in faith"), but I stress that poverty in the world's eyes, richness of faith, and inheriting the kingdom of God are appositional. James, as well as other biblical writers, points out God's pattern of choosing the lowly for divine mission. The lowly in society are the best exemplars of faith in God and hope for future restoration.

Divine election and associated promises are also common biblical concepts, starting with the Old Testament people of God and continuing into the New Testament.[8] James, with a call to "listen," "hear," or "be attentive" that is reminiscent of the opening of Israel's Shema (Deut 6:4), points to what the world cannot see: poverty and other forms of humiliation are not signs of divine

---

[6]See Dennis R. Edwards, *Might from the Margins: The Gospel's Power to Turn the Tables on Injustice* (Harrisonburg, VA: Herald Press, 2020).

[7]See, e.g., Pardue, *Mind of Christ*, 137-43. Pardue's discussion of feminists' and others' objections to the New Testament notion of kenosis applies to concerns about how humility and forgiveness might operate for marginalized people.

[8]For "election" see Deut 4:37-38; 7:7-8; Is 14:1; 43:10; cf. Acts 13:17; 1 Pet 1:2; 2:9; and for "promise" see Gen 28:4; Deut 1:8; cf. Mt 5:3—which may reflect the main source behind James's declaration.

alienation but are instead avenues that lead to divine restoration and vindication. In God's upside-down, topsy-turvy kingdom, those who have gained high position by playing the world's power games will be brought low, while those who have been alienated will be raised high. James makes this point later in the letter in his warning to rich oppressors:

> Come now, you rich people, weep and wail for the miseries that are coming to you. Your riches have rotted, and your clothes are moth-eaten. Your gold and silver have rusted, and their rust will be evidence against you, and it will eat your flesh like fire. You have laid up treasure for the last days. Listen! The wages of the laborers who mowed your fields, which you kept back by fraud, cry out, and the cries of the harvesters have reached the ears of the Lord of hosts. You have lived on the earth in luxury and in pleasure; you have fattened your hearts in a day of slaughter. You have condemned and murdered the righteous one, who does not resist you. (Jas 5:1-6)

Mary's song, after her visit from Gabriel, contains the same Old Testament themes that James reiterates:

> He has shown strength with his arm;
> he has scattered the proud in the thoughts of their hearts.
> He has brought down the powerful from their thrones,
> and lifted up the lowly;
> he has filled the hungry with good things,
> and sent the rich away empty. (Lk 1:51-53)

Those who have been humiliated are both invited and challenged to embrace their honored status in God's eyes. With the language of boasting, James has already pointed out how his perspective on humility works: "Let the believer who is lowly boast in being raised up, and the rich in being brought low, because the rich will disappear like a flower in the field" (Jas 1:9-10). One might argue that perception does not change reality, and that claiming honored status does not eliminate or mitigate oppression. However, women, ethnic minorities, the sexually alienated, the impoverished, and other humiliated people, who are able to receive divine favor in a unique way, can experience dimensions of joy and hope that others do not know.

Humble people are justifiably angry toward evil because they are attuned to injustice, and they also understand that dismantling unjust systems does not contradict but is a consequence of humility. Because humility is yielding to God and committing to peacemaking, it cannot equate to passivity. Marginalized people embody humility by focusing on the pain and alienation of others—not just their own—and joining in solidarity with the disinherited for the purpose of justice. We are most human when we admit our vulnerability and turn (repent) to rely on God's grace. Norman Wirzba observes,

> Humility is central to human life because it is through a humble attitude that we most fully approximate our true condition as creatures dependent on others, daily implicated in the life and death-wielding ways of creation, all together sustained by the gifts of our Creator. It is in terms of humility that we express the understanding that we do not stand alone or through our own effort; but live through the sacrifices and kindnesses of others.[9]

While the lowly of society, being rich in faith and heirs of God's kingdom, are exemplars of what it means to follow Jesus, they are more than merely resources for society's powerful people to

[9]Norman Wirzba, "The Touch of Humility: An Invitation to Creatureliness," *Modern Theology* 24, no. 2 (April 2008): 226.

consider emulating. Humble people are empowered to be the vessels through which God transforms individuals and communities.

The Muted Minister

Humility is central in the apostle Paul's letter to Philemon, even though the words *tapeinophrosynē* and *praus* do not appear.[10] Scholars debate the background of the letter, but most understand Onesimus to have been enslaved by Philemon.[11] Humility enables Philemon, the paterfamilias, to comply with Paul's request that Onesimus be welcomed "no longer as a slave but more than a slave, a beloved brother" (Philem 16). Likewise, Paul exercises humility throughout the letter, such as when he appeals to Philemon out of love and not authority (Philem 8-9). Michael J. Gorman examines Paul's words and presumed actions of the main characters in Philemon through the lens of *cruciformity* rather than humility, but the notions overlap, especially as Gorman puts Philippians 2:6-11 at the center of his argument.[12]

My focus here, however, is on muted Onesimus rather than Paul or Philemon. Most analyses of Paul's letter to Philemon focus on those two men, with Onesimus providing an opportunity for Philemon (and presumably the rest of the church) to learn and practice

---

[10]Colossians has often been linked to Philemon primarily because of the seven names the letters have in common: Timothy (Col 1:1; Philem 1), Epaphras (Col 1:7; 4:12; Philem 23), Aristarchus (Col 4:10; Philem 24), Mark (Col 4:10; Philem 24), Demas (Col 4:14; Philem 24), Archippus (Col 4:17; Philem 2), Luke (Col 4:14; Philem 24). In Colossians, false humility provides a contrast to genuine humility (Col 2:18, 23, vs. Col 3:12). If Paul wrote Colossians, then that letter would have accompanied or at least been delivered relatively close in time to Philemon's letter. Consequently, humility, which Paul expects of the entire church community in Colossae and is especially necessary for Onesimus and Philemon, is surely in the minds of all who heard Paul's words to Philemon.

[11]See Stephen E. Young, *Our Brother Beloved: Purpose and Community in Paul's Letter to Philemon* (Waco, TX: Baylor University Press, 2021), for a discussion of the most common views regarding Onesimus's backstory. Young does well to rescue Onesimus from the denigrating stereotypes associated with enslaved people, especially challenging the notion that Onesimus was a fugitive. Young suggests, along with some other scholars, that Philemon sent Onesimus on an errand to attend to Paul's needs in prison (see esp. 186-88).

[12]Michael J. Gorman, *Cruciformity: Paul's Narrative Spirituality of the Cross*, 20th anniversary ed. (Grand Rapids, MI: Eerdmans, 2021), 196-99.

reconciliation.[13] Onesimus, whose name means "useful" (see Philem 11), is a servant throughout the letter. Not only was he enslaved, but he also continues to serve Philemon by providing him an opportunity to put his faith in Jesus into action. Paul invites Philemon—vis-à-vis Onesimus—to put society's expectations into the background and Christian love into the foreground by freeing Onesimus and treating him as a Christian sibling (Philem 16).

Oppressive readings of Philemon included those supporting the United States' Fugitive Slave Act of 1850, which required enslaved people—even those who managed to get to a free state—to be returned to their enslavers. In light of slavery's legacy, recent interpreters have been giving greater attention to Paul's letter to Philemon, and African American scholars are at the forefront of newer studies, often paying greater attention to Onesimus. One especially poignant treatment is Matthew V. Johnson's essay "Onesimus Speaks: Diagnosing the Hys/Terror of the Text."[14] Johnson's work is challenging for many Bible readers because he refuses to assume "the preeminence of *Paul's* voice as being determinative for the approach to the text."[15] He further notes,

> If one takes seriously that God speaks in, to, and through the oppressed, then it seems to me only reasonable that God would be speaking to us in this text through Onesimus more so than Paul—particularly Onesimus as he comes to symbolize the silences in the text that nevertheless create tensions

[13]E.g., Norman R. Petersen, *Rediscovering Paul: Philemon and the Sociology of Paul's Narrative World* (Philadelphia: Fortress, 1985), 288-303, where Petersen focuses on "the closure of Paul's story about Philemon" (287) and how Paul's admonition is directed toward not only Philemon but also "the church that meets at Philemon's house, for the church itself will also have to receive the converted slave as a brother" (288).

[14]Matthew V. Johnson, "Onesimus Speaks: Diagnosing the Hys/Terror of the Text," in *Onesimus, Our Brother: Reading Religion, Race, and Culture in Philemon*, ed. Matthew V. Johnson, James A. Noel, and Demetrius K. Williams, Paul in Critical Contexts (Minneapolis, MN: Fortress, 2012), 91-100.

[15]Johnson, "Onesimus Speaks," 94.

that signify, so that he, like Abel, who was also murdered by his brother, "being dead yet speaketh" (Heb. 11:4).[16]

I have no intention of pitting Onesimus against Paul, or of offering a full critique of Johnson's essay. However, I appreciate that Johnson presses us to see that "Onesimus represents the terrible and earth-shattering silence, the disruptive spaces buried beneath the grand narratives of oppressive elites."[17] The lowly find a kindred spirit in Onesimus who is obviously to be counted among society's humiliated, but who may also be seen as humble. Onesimus's silence in the letter is not because Paul dishonors him but just the opposite—Paul honors Onesimus by leveraging the apostle's position with Philemon and the Christian community in Colossae and not requiring anything of Onesimus.[18]

Furthermore, perhaps Onesimus is silent because, having placed faith in Jesus Christ (Philem 10), he humbly trusts Paul to communicate on his behalf. Paul has positioned himself as *father* to Onesimus (Philem 10), who as an enslaved person would have had no legal status and whose own family situation was likely complicated or unstable.[19] Stephen E. Young makes

[16]Johnson, *Onesimus Speaks*, 97.

[17]Johnson, *Onesimus Speaks*, 95.

[18]Peter M. Head, "Onesimus the Letter Carrier and the Initial Reception of Paul's Letter to Philemon," *Journal of Theological Studies* 71, no. 2 (2020): 628-56, proffers that theory that Onesimus was the letter carrier and as such had the opportunity "to offer his voice and agency to the communication. It is the letter carrier who must resolve that which is unstated and ambiguous in the letter itself" (648).

[19]Young, *Our Brother Beloved*, 113. Young employs "Positioning Theory" to guide our understanding of the relational dynamics in Paul's letter to Philemon (62-63):

> Positioning Theory analyzes how people negotiate access to rights and duties in the process of conversation by positioning themselves or being positioned in relation to others, in light of developing (and at times competing) storylines, and within a particular context. In the case of the Letter to Philemon, virtually every sentence deals with complex dynamics of authority, power, status, rights, and duties within the community it envisions. Positioning Theory can be used as a tool, then, to identify how the letter as a communicative event positions the various participants in relation to each other, how in so doing it references the repertoire of storylines available both in its wider Greco-Roman context and within the local community it addresses, and how this serves to negotiate the issues of power, status, rights, and duties with which it is concerned.

clear that "whereas in the wider moral context of the empire Onesimus may have been legally fatherless, within the moral context of the church Paul has now become his father."[20] Onesimus humbly accepts the position as *child* to Paul, trusting that it will lead to his freedom and also to his position as *brother* to Philemon (Philem 16). Throughout the brief letter, Paul does not denigrate Onesimus.[21] Neither does Paul presume to speak for Onesimus by offering apologies on his behalf or stating Onesimus's loyalty to Philemon. Onesimus has not done anything wrong. In fact, Onesimus has demonstrated his usefulness for ministry (Philem 11).[22]

If Philemon is to follow through on Paul's request, then there will be a new relationship between Onesimus and Philemon. Privileged people tend to focus on the implications of this new family dynamic for Philemon rather than what it might mean for Onesimus. Philemon faced a dilemma concerning how he would treat an enslaved person who became a fellow Christian, but Onesimus demonstrates humility by returning to Philemon, trusting that he will be received as a full member of the Christian community. Onesimus's humility, evident in his "usefulness" in ministry and acceptance of the apostle Paul's leadership, leads to his relatively empowered position in society as a freeperson, as Philemon may have indeed manumitted Onesimus.[23] Also, Onesimus has been empowered to discover authentic Christian fellowship with Philemon and the saints in Colossae.

---

[20]Young, *Our Brother Beloved*, 115.

[21]Some scholars read Philem 18 through the lens of a familiar trope: an untrustworthy slave stealing from his master. However, the conditionality of the sentence, as well as the possible context, suggests that Onesimus need not be seen as a fugitive nor as a thief (Young, *Our Brother Beloved*, 147-56).

[22]Young, *Our Brother Beloved*, 116-18, equates the "formerly useless" of Philem 11 to "without Christ." Young's point is that with regard to Christian ministry, the unconverted Onesimus was useless, but with his conversion, that is no longer the case.

[23]Young, *Our Brother Beloved*, 201-5.

Turning Shame into Honor

Spiritual power comes from God and not from the world. This is to say that while we never ignore injustice, we cannot confuse influence in society with divine power. The Scriptures and history books are full of examples of people possessing worldly power who received their comeuppance. Babylonian king Belshazzar, featured in the infamous handwriting on the wall episode recorded in Daniel 5:1-31, is but one of many biblical examples of arrogant and mighty individuals who were taken down due to God's clear opposition, in the spirit of Proverbs 3:34. In fact, Daniel chastises Belshazzar for being haughty like his father Nebuchadnezzar (Dan 5:22), and essentially sentences him to an ignominious fate by saying, "You have exalted yourself against the Lord of heaven!" (Dan 5:23). Belshazzar is killed, and Darius the Mede takes over the kingdom (Dan 5:30-31). In more recent history, Adolf Hitler is one of numerous examples of prideful tyrants whose lives wrought terrible destruction but ended in disgrace. Both of those megalomaniacs, Belshazzar and Hitler, terrorized predominantly Jewish people but were eventually humiliated, with Hitler apparently committing suicide. There is no easy answer to why people like those men—and countless others—are allowed to wreak havoc for as long as they do, but eventually the warning of Proverbs 16:18 comes to pass:

> Pride goes before destruction,
> and a haughty spirit before a fall.

Humility empowers, but not always in the way the world expects. Worldly power has the potential for much good, but sin corrupts, leading to coercion, domination, and destruction. By contrast, divine power provides what is necessary to resist evil with perseverance and endurance, to be instrumental in overturning injustice, and to live as exemplars of persistent faith within a cynical society.

As noted in chapter six, 1 Peter is written to Christians who, because of their faith in Jesus Christ, are maligned and otherwise marginalized by their neighbors. The Christian community is suffering, and Peter addresses them as elect/chosen (1 Pet 1:2; 2:4, 6, 9), exiles (1 Pet 1:1; 2:11), strangers/aliens (1 Pet 2:11), part of a dispersion (1 Pet 1:1), and Christians (1 Pet 4:16). The broader society generally refuses to embrace exiles, aliens, and dispersed people, but uses them for entertainment or menial tasks. Such is the case in our North American context, evidenced in the treatment of Native Americans, enslaved Africans, and most immigrant groups. Minoritized people are forced to perform lowly work, receive unwarranted criticism, and at the same time provide comedic fodder for the majority culture. Even the artistic talents of marginalized people can get exploited for the benefit of those of higher status.

From a worldly perspective, each of the descriptors in 1 Peter—elect, alien, dispersed, Christian—can be heard as insults. These terms are negative identity markers that highlight detachment from the broader society. Even *elect*, being God's chosen people, a term meant to encourage the community, can provoke the ire of a society that does not honor God. People who claim to have a unique connection to God invite criticism and derision from others who view such claims as elitist. Peter, however, transforms insults into badges of honor. Peter takes terms that stigmatize and uses them as positive indicators of God's appreciation for believers who have been maligned by the world. Humility allows us to see ourselves as divine image bearers and empowers our self-identification, including redefining words that were used against us.

Shively T. J. Smith observes that

> the cosmology of 1 Peter functions as a narrative of knowledge in which diaspora is transformed from a punitive and embarrassing situation to a condition of being the legitimate people of God. Instead of titles such as "foreigner" and "Christian" being pejorative and limiting, the letter tells them to embrace these as markers of the diaspora-Christian situation.[24]

In 1 Peter 4:16, Peter tells his readers not to be ashamed if they suffer for having the title "Christian." The Greek noun *Christianos* is rare in the New Testament (also in Acts 11:26; 26:28), and most likely started as an epithet from critics of the Jesus movement.[25] David G. Horrell observes that

> the label Χριστιανός is a stigmatizing label associated not with a facet of personal identity—such as disability or disfigurement—but with a feature of social identity deriving from group membership. In relation to the term Χριστιανός, one thing that is interesting is that it is outsiders who heighten the salience of this label not only by coining it in the first place but also by making it, in judicial settings, *the* crucial identifier that determines whether a person is or is not a social deviant, whether they can be permitted to remain in society or not.[26]

Horrell considers the work of social science and suggests that the use of *Christianos* in 1 Peter 4:16 is an example of "the strategy of 'changing the values assigned to the attributes of the group, so that comparisons which were previously negative are now perceived as positive.' . . . In other words terms and designators with a

[24]Shively T. J. Smith, *Strangers to Family: Diaspora and 1 Peter's Invention of God's Household* (Waco, TX: Baylor University Press, 2016), 42.

[25]J. Ramsey Michaels, *1 Peter*, Word Biblical Commentary 49 (Grand Rapids, MI: Zondervan, 2015), 268-69. Michaels points out that the formation "Christian" is analogous to "Herodian," indicating "partisans of Christ" (268).

[26]David G. Horrell, "The Label Χριστιανός: 1 Peter 4:16 and the Formation of Christian Identity," *Journal of Biblical Literature* 126, no. 2 (2007): 377 (emphasis original).

negative social-identity value are retained, but reclaimed and re-interpreted, with what we may perhaps call polemical pride, as positive ones."[27] Peter encourages his readers to take what was considered a derogatory term and convert it into a badge of honor.

The power of humility is not about retaliation or fighting battles with worldly weapons. It is about embracing God's power to fight injustice in different ways. Part of the fight involves taking some of the satisfaction away from critics who attempt to cheapen us with their insults. Humility empowers God's people, particularly those who have been humiliated by the arrogant, to honor their true identity, even to the point of reappropriating language that was used against them.

Empowering in Practice

The term *introvert* long had a negative connotation, at least in most places where I heard it used, as people confused the term with shyness or weakness of character. Consequently, most of my life I was reluctant to acknowledge my introversion. Confessing my identity as an "introvert" would be taken as a sign of incapability or as some sort of personality defect.

When Susan Cain's *Quiet* was published, I eagerly listened to it as an audiobook.[28] It is hard to describe how invigorated I felt as I made my way through *Quiet*, recalling numerous instances in my life when I was made to feel inferior, weak, or simply odd because of my introversion. Cain's analysis helped me to see the benefits of introversion and gave me confidence to claim my identity as an introvert. I was empowered. Rather than accepting

[27]Horrell, "The Label Χριστιανός," 379 (emphasis original). The portion in single quotes is from Henri Tajfel and John Turner, "An Integrative Theory of Intergroup Conflict," in *Intergroup Relations: Essential Readings*, ed. Michael A. Hogg and Dominic Abrams (Philadelphia: Psychology Press, 2001), 104.

[28]Susan Cain, *Quiet: The Power of Introverts in a World That Can't Stop Talking* (New York: Broadway Paperbacks, 2013).

introvert as signaling a deficiency, I let it highlight my strengths. Not everyone understands introversion the way Cain described it. Some people might use *introvert* pejoratively, but I know better, and with knowledge there is power.

Such is the case with humility. Humility empowers not by changing circumstances or by changing other people, but by changing us. Humility allows us to see what God values, as in the case of the impoverished people in the book of James. As Paul's letter to Philemon anticipated, humility enables us to see a better way of relating to others that doesn't tolerate society's caste system. Humility empowers us to accept our countercultural identity and to reject marginalization by draining the life out of insults. Humility does not immediately bring about the divine reversals such as that announced in Mary's song (Lk 1:46-55), but it does help us access power that is greater than the worlds' power (see 1 Jn 4:4).

In the days of my youth, my people appropriated *Black* as a self-designation and turned what had been an insult into a cause for celebration. We sang the anthem from James Brown, "Say it loud; I'm Black and I'm proud" and found creative ways to assert, "Black is beautiful." To counter the dominant culture's demeaning messages, we honored our blackness and celebrated our accomplishments despite the nation's antagonism toward us. Currently, we declare that "Black lives matter" as part of our ongoing efforts to assert our dignity, declare our worth as fellow human beings, and keep ourselves safe from lynch mobs and the entire law enforcement system.

In addition to the countless biblical characters who humbly faced injustice, there are more recent heroes—perhaps in our own spheres of influence—who demonstrate humility's power. I regularly recall icons of America's civil rights movement and others like Nelson Mandela who fought against apartheid in South Africa. Yet even before that generation there were people like Ida B. Wells, who was born into slavery and became a journalist and antilynching crusader. Wells, who might have appeared lowly in the eyes of White people, was a giant who helped dismantle unjust systems. We might be tempted to consider the continuing struggle against injustice to be evidence of humility's uselessness, but perhaps we can also see that humility can be part of a subversive strategy for undermining powerbrokers.

It takes courage to be gentle and humble. Gentleness is a form of humility that stresses reliance on God rather than any atheistic human strength or ingenuity. We are able to be gentle when we realize not every encounter is a contest we must win. Gentleness restrains us from treating other humans with hatred or disrespect even when they are tools of injustice. Since the enemy of our souls is not flesh and blood (Eph 6:12), we refrain from demonizing other human beings. Courage is the ability to trust God to vindicate us, even when we have been humiliated (e.g., Rom 12:19). In the meantime, we strive for justice using every resource available to us without relying on violent retaliation (e.g., Rom 12:17; 1 Pet 3:9). Humble people do not deny the reality of injustice, but we confront it like Jesus did—with love and faith in God.

Conclusion

Humble yourselves therefore under the mighty hand of God, so that he may exalt you in due time.

1 Peter 5:6

One goal I had in writing this book was to provide a biblical analysis of a topic many people assume to be well-understood, and to explore its operation in Christian life. But perhaps every topic that an author writes about becomes the most important thing in their eyes. I became concerned that I'd see humility everywhere, even if it wasn't actually there.

However, while writing, I realized that much more could be said about humility, even in addition to what is in my bibliography. Also, I became increasingly convinced that by and large we either do not understand humility or we do understand it and are afraid to cultivate it. After all, if we were to embody the biblical humility that I attempted to describe, Christian praxis—at least in many settings—would be altered to the degree that it might no longer resemble what we have become accustomed to seeing. When compared to the self-centered, competitive society that we in the United States not only are used to but are largely convinced is what God intended, a life characterized by humility can appear too weak to make a difference for anyone or anything. We suspect that the kind of humility I advocate might make us too soft, too docile, too passive, and too insignificant. I imagine that our Christian forebears in the first century similarly wrestled with what it meant to participate in countercultural communities that conflicted with the competitive and coercive Roman world.

Yet, I'm naive enough to believe in humility's revival. I realize some of my evidence is anecdotal, but there are Christians fed up with power-hungry leaders inside and outside the church. Sometimes the righteous anger directed toward abusive leadership can turn into cynicism or skepticism, and some give up on Christian community altogether. But there are other Christians who are determined to be part of something different, something better, something more Christlike.

I am frequently invited to preach in churches and on college campuses, and often have the honor of meeting younger Jesus followers who believe that the Holy Spirit is working to reform God's church. Many of the younger people I meet have rejected the flashy, trendy, superficial, vain, and arrogant way Christianity has been practiced in various segments of our country, and they make me hopeful for the future. These people have not ignored the historical doctrinal concerns of the earlier days of Christianity, but they have rejected racist, homophobic, patriarchal, worldly ways that resonate to a greater degree with secular coercive powers than with the spiritual power that animates God's reign as seen in Jesus.

Other friends, Benjamin Byerly and his wife, Christi, whom I met in Washington, DC, demonstrate the way of humility even when it might have appeared risky. They have lived in a few different countries over the years, and I have had the pleasure of visiting them in Paris, France, and many years later in Nairobi, Kenya. In each city where I've connected with Ben and Christi, I've witnessed others honoring them for their generosity and humble service. There were times when people took advantage of their goodwill, yet Ben and Christi did not respond with vitriol or in ways that might denigrate those who exploited them. Instead, they continue to this day to be a family that welcomes strangers, serves without seeking accolades, and often treats others better than they get treated. This family has somehow discovered the power that comes through selfless giving.

There are ways that some Christians contribute to unhealthy division in our society. We have seen it in politics, the treatment of immigrants, in the ever-present racial tension in our country, and other areas. But it need not be that way. The world needs the presence of God to offer a foretaste of ultimate restoration that God promises (e.g., Rev 21:1-5). We who follow Jesus are empowered by the Holy Spirit to be agents of God's shalom, and humility undergirds all of our efforts. Humility does not ignore the antagonism, stubbornness, power-brokering, or denials that are part of our human existence—it confronts them. But humility confronts through dependence on the Holy Spirit instead of society's coercive strategies. Humble people submit to God honestly and wholeheartedly, accessing divine power to address human needs. I hope that you will be part of a growing movement of Christians who are not just disappointed with the status quo but who are also motivated afresh to live in the humble way of Jesus.

Blessed are the meek for they will inherit the land.

Bibliography

Alfeyev, Hilarion. *The Spiritual World of Isaac the Syrian*. Cistercian Studies 175. Kalamazoo, MI: Cistercian Publications, 2000.

Ashley, Timothy R. *The Book of Numbers*. New International Commentary on the Old Testament. Grand Rapids, MI: Eerdmans, 1993.

Augustine. *The City of God (De Civitate Dei)*. Introduction and Translation by William Babcock. Hyde Park, NY: New City Press, 1990.

———. *Confessions*. Translated by Sarah Ruden. New York: Modern Library, 2018.

Austin, Michael W. "Christian Humility as a Social Virtue." In *Character: New Directions from Philosophy, Psychology, and Theology*, edited by Christian B. Miller, R. Michael Furr, Angela Knobel, and William Fleeson, 333-50. New York: Oxford University Press, 2015.

———. *Humility and Human Flourishing: A Study in Analytic Moral Theology*. Oxford Studies in Analytic Theology. Oxford: Oxford University Press, 2018.

Austin, Michael W., and R. Douglas Geivett, eds. *Being Good: Christian Virtues for Everyday Life*. Grand Rapids, MI: Eerdmans, 2012.

Barclay, John M. G. "Food, Christian Identity and Global Warming: A Pauline Call for a Christian Food Taboo." *Expository Times* 121, no. 12 (2010): 585-93.

———. "Mirror-Reading a Polemical Letter: Galatians as a Test Case." In *The Galatians Debate: Contemporary Issues in Rhetorical and Historical Interpretation*, edited by Mark D. Nanos, 367-82. Peabody, MA: Hendrickson Publishers, 2002.

Beard, Mary. *SPQR: A History of Ancient Rome*. New York: Liveright, 2015.

Becker, Eve-Marie. *Paul on Humility*. Translated by Wayne Coppins. Baylor–Mohr Siebeck Studies in Early Christianity. Waco, TX: Baylor University Press, 2020.

Berlin, Adele, Marc Zvi Brettler, and Michael Fishbane, eds. *The Jewish Study Bible*. New York: Oxford University Press, 2004.

Bird, Michael F., and Nijay K. Gupta. *Philippians*. New Century Biblical Commentary. New York: Cambridge University Press, 2020.

Bonhoeffer, Dietrich. *Life Together: The Classic Exploration of Christian Community*. Translated by John W. Doberstein. San Francisco: HarperOne, 1993.

Budd, Philip J. *Numbers*. Word Biblical Commentary 5. Waco, TX: Word, 1984.

Burns, Lanier J. *Pride and Humility at War: A Biblical Perspective*. Phillipsburg, NJ: P&R, 2018.

Byron, Gay L. *Symbolic Blackness and Ethnic Difference in Early Christian Literature*. London: Routledge, 2002.

Byron, John. *Recent Research on Paul and Slavery*. Recent Research in Biblical Studies 3. Sheffield: Sheffield Phoenix Press, 2008.

Cain, Susan. *Quiet: The Power of Introverts in a World That Can't Stop Talking*. New York: Broadway Paperbacks, 2013.

Carroll, John T. *Luke: A Commentary*. New Testament Library. Louisville, KY: Westminster John Knox, 2012.

Cone, James. *A Black Theology of Liberation*. 40th anniversary ed. Maryknoll, NY: Orbis, 2010.

Constable, Harriet. "Sheep Are Not Stupid, and They Are Not Helpless Either." *The Independent*. April 27, 2017. https://m.theindependentbd.com/arcprint/details/91992/2017-04-27.

Creech, R. Robert. *Family Systems and Congregational Life: A Map for Ministry*. Grand Rapids, MI: Baker Academic, 2019.

Dawes, Stephen B. "*ʿĂnāwâ* in Translation and Tradition." *Vetus Testamentum* 41, no. 1 (January 1991): 38-48.

———. "Humility: Whence This Strange Notion?" *Expository Times* 103 (1991): 72-75.

———. "Walking Humbly: Micah 6:8 Revisited." *Scottish Journal of Theology* 41 (1988): 331-39,

deSilva, David A. *An Introduction to the New Testament: Contexts, Methods & Ministry Formation*. 2nd ed. Downers Grove, IL: IVP Academic, 2018.

DeYoung, Rebecca Konyndyk. *Vainglory: The Forgotten Vice*. Grand Rapids, MI: Eerdmans, 2014.

Dickson, John P. *Humilitas: A Lost Key to Life, Love, and Leadership*. Grand Rapids, MI: Zondervan, 2011.

Dickson, John P., and Brian S. Rosner. "Humility as a Social Virtue in the Hebrew Bible?" *Vetus Testamentum* 54, no. 4 (2004): 459-79.

Douglas, Kelly Brown, and Delbert Burkett. "The Black Christ." In *The Blackwell Companion to Jesus,* edited by Delbert Burkett, 410-26. Blackwell Companions to Religion. Malden, MA: Wiley-Blackwell, 2011.

Dunn, James D. G. *The Epistle to the Galatians*. Black's New Testament Commentary. 1993. Reprint, Grand Rapids, MI: Baker Academic, 2011.

———. *Romans 9–16*. Word Biblical Commentary 38B. Dallas: Word, 1988.

Dunnington, Kent. *Humility, Pride, and Christian Virtue Theory*. Oxford Studies in Analytic Theology. New York: Oxford University Press, 2019.

Eddy, Mary Baker. *Science and Health with Key to the Scriptures*. Boston: Christian Science Publishing Company, 1875. www.christianscience.com/the-christian-science-pastor/science-and-health.

Edwards, Dennis R. "Colossians and Philemon." In *The New Testament in Color*, edited by Esau McCaulley, Janette H. Ok, Osvaldo Padilla, and Amy L. B. Peeler. Downers Grove, IL: IVP Academic, forthcoming.

———. *1 Peter*. Story of God Bible Commentary. Grand Rapids, MI: Zondervan, 2017.

———. "Guarding the Flock." In *Living the King Jesus Gospel: Discipleship and Ministry Then and Now*, edited by Nijay K. Gupta, Tara Beth Leach, Matthew W. Bates, and Drew J. Strait, 80-96. Eugene, OR: Cascade, 2021.

———. *Might from the Margins: The Gospel's Power to Turn the Tables on Injustice*. Harrisonburg, VA: Herald Press, 2020.

———. "Slave, Slavery," in *Dictionary of Paul and His Letters*. Edited by Scot McKnight, Lynn H. Cohick, and Nijay K. Gupta. 2nd edition. Downers Grove, IL: IVP Academic, 2023.

Edwards, Korie L. *The Elusive Dream: The Power of Race in Interracial Churches*. 2nd ed. Oxford University Press, 2021.

Elliott, John H. *1 Peter: A New Translation with Introduction and Commentary*. Anchor Bible 37B. New York: Doubleday, 2000.

Fee, Gordon D. *Paul's Letter to the Philippians*. New International Commentary on the New Testament. Grand Rapids, MI: Eerdmans, 1995.

Feldmeier, Reinhard. *Power, Service, Humility: A New Testament Ethic*. Waco, TX: Baylor University Press, 2014.

Fitzmyer, Joseph A. *The Acts of the Apostles*. Anchor Bible 31. New York: Doubleday, 1998.

———. *First Corinthians: A New Translation with Introduction and Commentary*. Anchor Bible 32. New Haven, CT: Yale University Press, 2008.

———. *The Gospel According to Luke: Introduction, Translation, and Notes*. Anchor Bible 28A. Garden City, NY: Doubleday, 1981.

———. *Romans: A New Translation with Introduction and Commentary*. Anchor Bible 33. New York: Doubleday, 1993.

Fodor, Jim. "Christian Discipleship as Participative Imitation: Theological Reflections on Girardian Themes." In *Violence Renounced: René Girard, Biblical Studies, and Peacemaking*, edited by Willard M. Swartley, 246-76. Studies in Peace and Scripture 4. Telford, PA: Pandora Press, 2000.

Foulcher, Jane. *Reclaiming Humility: Four Studies in the Monastic Tradition*. Cistercian Studies 255. Collegeville, MN: Cistercian Publications, 2015.

Fowl, Stephen E., and L. Gregory Jones. *Reading in Communion. Scripture and Ethics in Christian Life*. Grand Rapids, MI: Eerdmans, 1991.

Gamble, Harry Y. "Literacy and Book Culture." In *Dictionary of New Testament Background: A Compendium of Contemporary Biblical Scholarship*, edited by Stanley E. Porter and Craig A. Evans, 644-48. Downers Grove, IL: IVP Academic, 2000.

Gaventa, Beverly Roberts. *Our Mother Saint Paul*. Louisville, KY: Westminster John Knox, 2007.

Gilliard, Frank D. "More Silent Reading in Antiquity: *Non Omne Verbum Sonabat*." *Journal of Biblical Literature* 112, no. 4 (1993): 689-94.

Goheen, Michael W., and Michael D. Williams. "Doctrine of Scripture and Theological Interpretation." In *A Manifesto for Theological Interpretation*, edited by Craig G. Bartholomew and Heath A. Thomas, 48-71. Grand Rapids, MI: Baker Academic, 2016.

Gorman, Michael J. *Apostle of the Crucified Lord: A Theological Introduction to Paul and His Letters*. 2nd ed. Grand Rapids, MI: Eerdmans, 2016.

———. *Cruciformity: Paul's Narrative Spirituality of the Cross*. Grand Rapids, MI: Eerdmans, 2001.

Gorringe, Tim. "Rise Peter! Kill and Eat: A Response to John Barclay." *Expository Times* 123, no. 2 (2011): 63-69.

Grant, Michael. *The Twelve Caesars*. New York: Scribner, 1975.

Graves, Marlena. *The Way Up Is Down: Becoming Yourself by Forgetting Yourself*. Downers Grove, IL: InterVarsity Press, 2020.

Guinn, Jeff. *The Road to Jonestown: Jim Jones and Peoples Temple*. New York: Simon & Schuster, 2017.

Gupta, Nijay K. *1 & 2 Thessalonians*. Zondervan Critical Introductions to the New Testament. Grand Rapids, MI: Zondervan, 2019.

Hamilton, Victor P. *The Book of Genesis: Chapters 1–17*. New International Commentary on the Old Testament. Grand Rapids, MI: Eerdmans, 1990.

Hawthorne, Gerald F. *Philippians*. Word Biblical Commentary 43. Waco, TX: Word, 1987.

Hays, Richard B. *Reading Backwards: Figural Christology and the Fourfold Gospel Witness*. Waco, TX: Baylor University Press, 2014.

Head, Peter M. "Onesimus the Letter Carrier and the Initial Reception of Paul's Letter to Philemon." *Journal of Theological Studies* 71, no. 2 (2020): 628-56.

Hellerman, Joseph H. *Embracing Shared Ministry: Power and Status in the Early Church and Why It Matters Today*. Grand Rapids, MI: Kregel, 2013.

Herman, Judith Lewis. *Trauma and Recovery*. New York: Basic Books, 2015.

Holmes, Michael W., trans. *The Apostolic Fathers: Greek Texts and English Translations*. 2nd ed. Grand Rapids, MI: Baker Books, 1999.

Horrell, David G. "The Label Χριστιανός: 1 Peter 4:16 and the Formation of Christian Identity." *Journal of Biblical Literature* 126, no. 2 (2007): 361-81.

Horrell, David G., Cherryl Hunt, and Christopher Southgate. *Greening Paul: Rereading the Apostle in a Time of Ecological Crisis*. Waco, TX: Baylor University Press, 2010.

Hutchinson, Christopher. *Rediscovering Humility: Why the Way Up Is Down*. Greensboro, NC: New Growth Press, 2018.

Johnson, Luke Timothy. *The Letter of James: A New Translation with Introduction and Commentary.* Anchor Bible 37A. New York: Doubleday, 1995.

Johnson, Matthew V. "Onesimus Speaks: Diagnosing the Hys/Terror of the Text." In *Onesimus, Our Brother: Reading Religion, Race, and Culture in Philemon*, edited by Matthew V. Johnson, James A. Noel, and Demetrius K. Williams, 91-100. Paul in Critical Contexts. Minneapolis, MN: Fortress, 2012.

Jones, Kirk Byron. *Rest in the Storm: Self-Care Strategies for Clergy and Other Caregivers.* Valley Forge, PA: Judson Press, 2021.

Keener, Craig S. *Acts: An Exegetical Commentary*. Grand Rapids, MI: Baker Academic, 2012.

———. *Galatians: A Commentary*. Grand Rapids, MI: Baker Academic, 2018.

Kent, Dan. *Confident Humility: Becoming Your Full Self without Becoming Full of Yourself.* Minneapolis, MN: Fortress, 2018.

Kidner, Derek. *Psalms 1–72. Tyndale Old Testament Commentary*. Downers Grove, IL: InterVarsity Press, 1973.

Kivel, Paul. *Uprooting Racism: How White People Can Work for Racial Justice*. Rev. ed. Gabriola Island, BC: New Society Publishers, 2002.

Kvanvig, Jonathan L. *Faith and Humility*. Oxford: Oxford University Press, 2018.

Linzey, Andrew. *Animal Theology*. London: SCM Press, 1994.

Maier, Harry O. *Picturing Paul in Empire: Imperial Image, Text and Persuasion in Colossians, Ephesians and the Pastoral Epistles*. London: Bloomsbury, 2013.

Martin, Clarice J. "The *Haustafeln* (Household Codes) in African American Interpretation: 'Free Slaves' and 'Subordinate Women.'" In *Stony the Road We Trod: African American Biblical Interpretation*, edited by Cain Hope Felder, 206-31. Minneapolis, MN: Fortress, 1991.

Mays, James Luther. *Micah: A Commentary*. Old Testament Library. Philadelphia: Westminster, 1976.

McCarter, P. Kyle, Jr. *I Samuel: A New Translation*. Anchor Bible 8. Garden City, NY: Doubleday, 1980.

McKnight, Scot. *A Fellowship of Differents: Showing the World God's Design for Life Together*. Grand Rapids, MI: Zondervan, 2015.

———. *The Letter of James*. New International Commentary on the New Testament. Grand Rapids, MI: Eerdmans, 2011.

———. *The Letter to Philemon*. New International Commentary on the New Testament. Grand Rapids, MI: Eerdmans, 2017.

———. *The Letter to the Colossians*. New International Commentary on the New Testament. Grand Rapids, MI: Eerdmans, 2018.

———. *Reading Romans Backwards: A Gospel of Peace in the Midst of Empire*. Waco, TX: Baylor University Press, 2019.

———. *Sermon on the Mount*. Story of God Bible Commentary 21. Grand Rapids, MI: Zondervan, 2013.

Merton, Thomas. *No Man Is an Island*. Boston: Shambhala, 2005.

Michaels, J. Ramsey. *1 Peter.* Word Biblical Commentary 49. Grand Rapids, MI: Zondervan, 2015.

Mills, Charles W. *The Racial Contract*. Ithaca, NY: Cornell University Press, 1997.

Mofokeng, Takatso Alfred. *The Crucified Among the Crossbearers: Towards a Black Christology.* Kampen: Kok, 1983.

Moo, Douglas J., and Jonathan A. Moo. *Creation Care: A Biblical Theology of the Natural World*. Biblical Theology for Life. Grand Rapids, MI: Zondervan, 2018.

Murray, Andrew. *Humility*. Springdale, PA: Whitaker House, 1982.

NAACP. "Criminal Justice Fact Sheet." Accessed February 15, 2023. www.naacp.org/criminal-justice-fact-sheet/.

O'Brien, Julia M. *Nahum, Habakkuk, Zephaniah, Haggai, Zechariah, Malachi.* Abingdon Old Testament Commentaries. Nashville: Abingdon, 2004.

Packer, David. "The Cows Are in the Corn." *Medium*, November 15, 2009. https://medium.com/nighttimethoughts/the-cows-are-in-the-corn-8b67779ab21a.

Papanikolaou, Aristotle. "Person, Kenosis and Abuse: Hans Urs von Balthasar and Feminist Theologies in Conversation." *Modern Theology* 19, no. 1 (2003): 41-65.

Pardue, Stephen T. *The Mind of Christ: Humility and the Intellect in Early Christian Theology*. T&T Clark Studies in Systematic Theology 23. London: Bloomsbury T&T Clark, 2013.

Petersen, Norman R. *Rediscovering Paul: Philemon and the Sociology of Paul's Narrative World*. Philadelphia: Fortress, 1985.

Peterson, Eugene. *Leap Over a Wall: Earthy Spirituality for Everyday Christians.* New York: HarperCollins, 1997.

Pew Research Center. "Blacks and Hispanics Are Overrepresented in U.S. Prisons." January 12, 2018. www.pewresearch.org/fact-tank/2019/04/30/shrinking-gap-between-number-of-blacks-and-whites-in-prison/ft_18-01-10_prisonracegaps_2/.

Pohl, Christine D. *Making Room: Recovering Hospitality as a Christian Tradition*. Grand Rapids, MI: Eerdmans, 1999.

Pokorný, Petr. *Colossians: A Commentary*. Peabody, MA: Hendrickson, 1991.

Rutledge, Fleming. "Reading the Bible in Worship for the Renewal of the Church." Generous Orthodoxy, September 8, 2021. https://generousorthodoxy.org/rumination/reading-the-bible-in-worship-for-the-renewal-of-the-church.

Scheepers, John. "How Did Our 'Good Evangelical Theology' Allow Apartheid?" Isiphambano Centre for Biblical Justice, October 22, 2018. https://www.isiphambano.com/blog/how-did-our-good-evangelical-theology-allow-apartheid.

Skehan, Patrick W., and Alexander A. Di Lella. *The Wisdom of Ben Sira: A New Translation with Notes*. Anchor Bible 39. New York: Doubleday, 1987.

Smith, Mitzi. "Slavery." In *True to Our Native Land: An African-American New Testament Commentary*, edited by Brian K. Blount, Cain Hope Felder, Clarice J. Martin, and Emerson B. Powery, 11-22. Minneapolis, MN: Fortress, 2007.

Smith, Shively T. J. *Strangers to Family: Diaspora and 1 Peter's Invention of God's Household*. Waco, TX: Baylor University Press, 2016.

Standish, N. Graham. *Humble Leadership: Being Radically Open to God's Guidance and Grace*. Herndon, VA: Alban Institute, 2007.

Suetonius. *The Twelve Caesars*. Translated by Robert Graves. Penguin Classics. New York: Penguin, 2003.

Tajfel, Henri, and John Turner. "An Integrative Theory of Intergroup Conflict." In *Intergroup Relations: Essential Readings*, edited by Michael A. Hogg and Dominic Abrams, 94-109. Philadelphia: Psychology Press, 2001.

Thompson, Marianne Meye. *Colossians and Philemon*. Two Horizons New Testament Commentary. Grand Rapids, MI: Eerdmans, 2005.

Thorsteinsson, Runar M. *Roman Christianity and Roman Stoicism: A Comparative Study of Ancient Morality*. New York: Oxford University Press, 2010.

Thurman, Howard. *Jesus and the Disinherited*. 1949. Reprint, Boston: Beacon, 1996.

Volf, Miroslav. *The End of Memory: Remembering Rightly in a Violent World*. Grand Rapids, MI: Eerdmans, 2006.

Walker, Michael A. "Persistent Pain and Promised Perfection: The Significance of an Embodied Eschatology of Disability." *Journal of Disability and Religion* 27, no. 2 (2023): 108-23.

Walker-Barnes, Chanequa. *I Bring the Voices of My People: A Womanist Vision for Racial Reconciliation*. Prophetic Christianity. Grand Rapids, MI: Eerdmans, 2019.

Wallace, Daniel B. *Greek Grammar Beyond the Basics: An Exegetical Syntax of Grammar*. Grand Rapids, MI: Zondervan, 1997.

Waltke, Bruce K. *The Book of Proverbs: Chapters 15–31*. New International Commentary on the Old Testament. Grand Rapids, MI: Eerdmans, 2005.

Walton, Jonathan. *Twelve Lies That Hold America Captive: And the Truth That Sets Us Free*. Downers Grove, IL: InterVarsity Press, 2018.

Wengst, Klaus. *Humility: Solidarity of the Humiliated; The Transformation of an Attitude and Its Social Relevance in Graeco-Roman, Old Testament-Jewish, and Early Christian Tradition*. Translated by John Bowden. Philadelphia: Fortress, 1988.

Wenham, Gordon J. *Numbers: An Introduction and Commentary*. Tyndale Old Testament Commentary. Downers Grove, IL: InterVarsity Press, 1981.

Whitson, William, trans. *The Works of Josephus: Complete and Unabridged*. Peabody, MA: Hendrickson, 1988.

Wilkerson, Isabel. *Caste: The Origins of Our Discontents*. New York: Random House, 2020.

Wirzba, Norman. "The Touch of Humility: An Invitation to Creatureliness." *Modern Theology* 24, no. 2 (2008): 225-44.

Works, Carla Swafford. *The Least of These: Paul and the Marginalized*. Grand Rapids, MI: Eerdmans, 2019.

Wright, Brian J. *Communal Reading in the Time of Jesus: A Window into Early Christian Reading Practices*. Minneapolis, MN: Fortress, 2017.

Wright, Catherine J. *Spiritual Practices of Jesus: Learning Simplicity, Humility, and Prayer with Luke's Earliest Readers*. Downers Grove, IL: IVP Academic, 2020.

Wright, Jennifer Cole, ed. *Humility*. The Virtues: Multidisciplinary Perspectives. New York: Oxford University Press, 2019.

Wright, N. T. *Paul and the Faithfulness of God*. Minneapolis, MN: Fortress Press, 2013.

Young, Stephen E. *Our Brother Beloved: Purpose and Community in Paul's Letter to Philemon*. Waco, TX: Baylor University Press, 2021.

Scripture Index

Missio Alliance

Missio Alliance has arisen in response to the shared voice of pastors and ministry leaders from across the landscape of North American Christianity for a new "space" of togetherness and reflection amid the issues and challenges facing the church in our day. We are united by a desire for a fresh expression of evangelical faith, one significantly informed by the global evangelical family. Lausanne's Cape Town Commitment, "A Confession of Faith and a Call to Action," provides an excellent guidepost for our ethos and aims.

Through partnerships with schools, denominational bodies, ministry organizations, and networks of churches and leaders, Missio Alliance addresses the most vital theological and cultural issues facing the North American church in God's mission today. We do this primarily by convening gatherings, curating resources, and catalyzing innovation in leadership formation.

Rooted in the core convictions of evangelical orthodoxy, the ministry of Missio Alliance is animated by a strong and distinctive theological identity that emphasizes

Comprehensive Mutuality: Advancing the partnered voice and leadership of women and men among the beautiful diversity of the body of Christ across the lines of race, culture, and theological heritage.

Hopeful Witness: Advancing a way of being the people of God in the world that reflects an unwavering and joyful hope in the lordship of Christ in the church and over all things.

Church in Mission: Advancing a vision of the local church in which our identity and the power of our testimony is found and expressed through our active participation in God's mission in the world.

In partnership with InterVarsity Press, we are pleased to offer a line of resources authored by a diverse range of theological practitioners. The resources in this series are selected based on the important way in which they address and embody these values, and thus, the unique contribution they offer in equipping Christian leaders for fuller and more faithful participation in God's mission.